Late Night Poets Anthology

Volume 2

Edited By:

Fillmyeyes

Anthology Volume 2

DEDICATION

To All The Wonderful People of
Late Night Poets Group on Allpoetry.com

Let Us Not Forget…

Rock a Little

Gill Blaze

Jocvaughan

ACKNOWLEDGMENTS

I would like to thank everyone that helped me with this project.
To Deb, Pam & M. K. For the long, long sleepless nights as I talked to myself while you sat
there just listening to my yammer ☺ To Laurent for all the guidance and editing advice.
I know I was tough to work with, Thank you for your patience.
Much Love to each of you.
Last But Never Ever Least
Thank you "D"
You are a great friend!

CONTENTS

Luyu Wild Dove
Garden of Enlightenment

Blossoming Syrupy Nectar
By: Luyu Wild Dove

wet tongue,
hardened tipped breasts
slippery, sliding, creamed,
rubbed orgastic drenched skin,
ambered macadamia, glistening oil

smearing breathing, endowed buttery lips,
flavoring skin,
ginger, vanilla sugared suckled fingers
aquamarine igneous ablaze eyesight,
juicy scented petals spread
blossoming syrupy nectar
water's pollinating elixir

ambrosial marigolds beneath satin pillows,
peppermint finger-play awakenings
pleading nibbling, slurping sassafras streams, paralyzing, shivering
whispering, "lend, your unripened repertoire."
begging, sandal wood tangs, sips
stopping, murmuring, sliding up,
distilling our blending libido,
smelling steamy ginger spices, exhaled vapours,
swirling tongues heated in honied wine,
feasting liquids

Some libraries require overhauls; I just needed a new book
By: Ademon

I replaced you with books
because my spine grew tired
from cracking every time
you opened me
as if I'd ever let you
become yesterday's graffiti
within these subway tiled bones

you told me writers are
desperate people
and when the desperation fades
so do the writers with no second thoughts
it's just the status quo
the unapologetic blanket of solidarity

there was a time
where I would have wished
that to be true but

these scars are not invisible
and the exhausted trees sway
in that forgotten city
you scorched with every
exhale you gave my name

I remember each scream whispered
through angry syllables
and how they scarred our throats
the rage of a scorned storm tearing
at every corner of this sky

I know you didn't notice
my withering smile
you were too busy
painting someone else's

The Lady Of The Forest
By: Adrian Bravos

I am the lady of the forest.
And I speak for the creatures that lurk within.

I am the guardian of those who cannot fend for themselves.
I am the wind that makes the trees sway.

I am the lady of the forest.
And I speak for the creatures that lurk within.

I am the one who protects this forest from intruders like you.
I am the one who dresses the leaves in morning dew.

I am the lady of the forest
And I speak for the creatures within.

I am the flowers that spring up from the decaying bones of trees.
I am the soft breeze that carries the bees.

I am the lady of the forest.
And I speak for the creatures that lurk within.

I am the queen of the creatures of these sacred woods
I am the one who sees through all your falsehoods.

I am the lady of the forest
And I speak for the creatures that lurk within.

Natures Gain
By: Adrian41062

The disused rail line
Feels so cold in wintertime
the sunny, foggy, hazy, hue
the silouhette of a deer walking through

Snow laden across the track
will it's history ever be brought back?
locomotives of the steamage gone
overgrown, a relic this has become

I walk in the solitude, the peace I see
squirrels dancing up a tree
partridge, pheasant I come across
natures gain histories loss

You Deserve Better
By: Afeezee

You deserve better like
the rose with thorny stem.

You deserve better like
the lonely seed in the pear's pod.

You deserve better like
the lonely star, 1500 light years
from its nearest neighbour.

You deserve better like
a house with no roof.

You are the pineapple
supported by sturdy stem
but alone you stand
looking for your likes.

The whale's loud noise
longing for his closest mate
shakes the ocean like
it is a sign of horror.

Don't Go Down There
By: Agressman

I grin at speckled minnows
under the bruises
that ripened in layered
faded flashlights
flickering yellow light.
Corroded arteries
within white aluminum springs
baying terrazzo flecks.

Caked on dirt in crevices
weeding halos on basement
bricks of pariahs, bottling
serpentine memories
warped by towering
ferrymen.

Leathered torsos
spitting blindly
triangular snowflakes
that yield red budded
follicles of grooved
warmth onto
bulbous buttocks.

Tick-tock weathered
rhythmic beats
of laundry spinning
eyes clenching
white light,
turtled
in a corner.

OMG
By: Agressman

I looked into the car window and saw death,
in the shape of a petite woman with a cell phone.
Steering the car with her knees, texting,
driving while deeply engrossed in a conversation
with her coworker on the merits of Paid Time Off.
The air became still and silent as the fender
accordioned and shards of plastic became
lords a leaping.

The shock quickly trumpeted the air bag
into action and the force quickly delivered my arm
through the window like a salute to a fallen dictator.
My torso became twisted as the steering wheel
collapsed and my ankle became the Aleutian
island chain of calamity, with knees buckled
like 70 shoes.

My legs became dangling participles of
puppets without strings, and my eyes traced
diamonds that wrote blank checks of urban sprawl.
Faded whispers fell to the Wah Wah of the ambulance.
I was lifted by pelicans to the ferry docks,
drained of fear and placed on the clothesline to dry.
Lights hummed hallelujah, and the ping ping ping
grabbed the crow eyes attention.

The petite lady conversed with the bandanna
pirate that sipped on a caramel macchiato while
distorted voices yelled clear the gang plank,
we've arranged for the whirly bird to land.
Impressions were firmly seated to the left of
the ghost, as I raised my bird to fly its last time.

Inconvenienced motorists grabbed the horror
through digital pictures, did you get my best side?
Ripped from life, like pages of 30 year old
readers digest where crosswords puzzles,
we left unfinished. Her phone was found,
with the last text frozen, OMG.

Two Pac
By: Amancie

" One who choose to be heard
picks the right words,
Then allow them too spurge!!

" Words can man you up
or made to become
corrupt.

" Gently puffing on some leaves
and kicking the breezes.
Allowing your mind to feel thoses
magical keys.(Which is Music)

It's like preaching and teaching
to your fans.
And delivering a personal
self-check, Others will feel the
reflects and denied your checks.

" Plus the Academy Awards
your lyrics don't set with
the board....

" But you and your Mother
say leave it all to lord,
Cause, I lived my life with
a doublesword...

" All Eye's On Me !!

That Feeling
By: Andreas68

That Feeling
Maybe it's the...

snow-capped mountains piercing the clouds with their magnificence

tall green pines that have been here since before
Columbus's birth and are over thirty stories high

roaring rivers cascading down the mountainside
to the valley below with its salmon defying logic and odds

rocky ledges so subtly shaped by glaciers thousands of years ago

smells of the ocean air that greets you in the morning

pods of killer whales playing alongside the island ferry

sea faring going vessel like a ghost ship on its way to parts unknown

sights of a soaring eagle gliding oh so effortlessly through the blue skies

sounds of a baby deer born within earshot of a friend

fragrances exuded by the myriad of flowers of varying shapes and colors

sunrise and sunset that makes you gaze in awe

open arms that greet you when you return home

And that feeling, it is the knowing that you are exactly
where you are meant to be

I've always wanted
By: Andre de Korvin

To write a poem where rivers flow
free as my verse
and high rises drown in purple

and gold waves of the sun.
I've always wanted to write a poem
where children shape

smiling faces in the mud.
A poem where weeping willows
shake their green heads, cheerfully

gazing into the blue
hazy mirror of the sky.
Sipping coffee, I look

through my many windows
and wait for a poem
to drive by.

Although sunlight is everywhere
and moody cups throw halos
like saints handing in their resignation,

street lights bow their heads,
their eyes scanning every direction
hoping for night to come soon.

I drink my coffee black,
and lean over the white table
and although the room

is brightly lit,
my head filling up
with unwritten stanzas

throws starless nights
across that white table,
and the crumpled pages of my draft.

Consume Me
By Angeleyez

Consume Me

Close your eyes,
reach out with the
tendrils of your soul.
Pull mine close, bathe
in my essence.

Rest, in my peace.
Sleep, in my comfort.
Rage, with my anger.
Sit, in my silence.
Mourn, in my despair.

Feel, the merriment, in
my conquests.
Grasp, the courage, in
my challenges.
Clutch, the shame, in my failures.
See, the opportunities,
in my defeats.

Glimpse, the jubilation,
in my smile.
Taste, the passion, when
you drink from my lips.
Feel, my lungs, expand
as I breathe you in.

All Of I
By AngelHaze

I need someone either fake or true,
I need someone that gets me through.

I need my brother, my pride,
I need my sister by my side.

I need a friend close and dear,
I need a hand to cast away my fear.

I need you to help me heal,
I need you before i forget how to feel.

I need her eyes to stop crying,
I need my soul to stop dying .

I need the voices to stop screaming,
I need the dreams to stop dreaming.

I need your secret fire,
I need your flames of desire.

I need to end and restart,
I need to leave it all behind me and depart.

I need to turn down the lights,
I need your shadow to rule my nights.

I need you in the end,
All I need is a friend.

Wandering Yesterdays
By: Anguish

He wanders

"neath the gelid warmth

of yesterday's eclipse,

imbibing the scent

of nevermore

as leaves of mem'ry

      tremble

'pon the brittle bones

of broken promises

clinging 'midst the remnants

he's locked in reliquary.

His quietude echoes

sombre dirge,

a masticated melody

of meaning lost

left to mingle 'midst his road

of rusted reasons

and yet, he knows

he'll mourn it's tragic loss

when nostalgia fades to black.....

Autumn's Road
By: Anguish

As crimson leaves eclipse the tar

they rustle peacefully,

Beneath the breath of zephyr breeze

That whiffs so blissfully,

While rain in hues of Autumn's kiss

Sashays from Laden trees,

To light upon the quilted earth

Where memories will freeze.

Beneath a sky of azure shades

Imbued of algid air,

The arms of nature's stalwart guards

Protect its woundrous lair,

While fences walk her shoulder's curve

In search of human strays,

And sunset guilds the cherished hues

Before it fades away.

The season splays emblazoned glow

Awaiting winter's wrath,

While rainbows grace with fall pelisse

Upon the winding path,

Where luchious foliage waits to fade

Within the cold, forbode,

And sights of splendor hypnotize

Upon the Autumn Road.

M.K. Rock
Tuesday's Timepieces

inspiration flutters against the bone of brick
By: M.K. Rock

her eye teeth were first cut
on indigestible syllables,
chunks chewed to soften fit;

faith and fury stepped squarely
onto designation's mark,
                park poetry here;

she gathered autumn's russet,
saffron foliage, and winged spice,
            swirled in afternoon's alarm
tragic suffering,
quest curried lines finely combed;

ink swaths, pulled laufly to surround her,
puncturing sensitive poetic tegument,
steeped in tuesday's episteme;

there is no sense to be made of madness...
she sifts ruins of rampage,
through a brittle rustle of branched reaches;

fingertips eager to steal from harrowing headlines,
earned by four wheeled hatred,
hawked in printed cries of pedestrian cull;

shock and wisdom temper angry musings,
text tossed to october floss,
frost drifts east too soon;

mukluks fail to warm footprints,
lost in stormed depths, adapting to odd angles;
mending sorrows, are absorbed in the rush

thrum of a busy neighborhood pulse;
meter flutters arterials, emergent rhythms of her beat

urging stained pains to seek flight.

The Artist
By: Anton Ansford

Nature is like all great artists:
rearranging the elements
to suit our human eyes
the canvas the plains, seas and skies

Each day the palette changes
One day:Mauves, pinks and oranges,
the next, red, vermillion and scarlets, beginning, as the sun sets,
with differentiated shades and hue
but ending in one Watery pink or blue

Today, the Artist has chosen a costly gold,
as if king midas has pranced around the land before realizing the deadly price of
his wishes.

White Falcon 500
By: A P Taylor

Thick blood gurgled in my
father's veins, and became dirtier
with age. The viscous debris
of once eaten steaks, overtaking
his broken insides.

Oil thickens without draining,
parts then begin failing. Same as
the falcon car when he sold it.
Lying for scrap and five hundred
dollars in a wrecking yard.

His engine no warranty,
carburettor rough. A mouth
seeking air in gallons,
eyes coffin pale. Loud deep
breaths, an echoing rattle.

My call at night, arriving
to eyes frozen. As a piece of
marble, Moore like, carved mid
breath. Wrinkled face
stared, slate grey,

Halogen lights on his
frozen frame. A part turned
key in an ignition, stuck.
Imprint bent to a concave
circular shape.

Stood,
held all,
paused,
floated and
backed up into the lift.

Into the hollow darkness
of a storm hovering.
Silently an empty shadow
looked upon, sat on my
shoulder and pressed down.

In this cloud the minutiae of
grief in family, newspapers,
programs, urns, papers,
speeches and programs to
"remember, held near."

Childhood memories seeped,
years listening to his records.
Assorted sixties country and pop.
And I began a journey, to a
record player spinning.

Soaring echoes took me to
the Falcon on a road trip.
Refrains, matched plains,
strident saxophones the
rustling grasslands.

To a bitumen road and him sitting,
driving. Singing in his tenor voice a
chorus, "you gave me a mountain".
By the rear view I glimpsed his eyes,
fiery hazel, matching mine

Flames of Passion
By: As3mis

Wild flames waltz
during winter solstice
to the silent, throbbing beat
of coals pulsating beneath them.

Twinkling stars wink
as the breeze feeds smoke
being released from where
they luminously dance.

A full moon glares down
at the aura of sparks around the fire
as embers sizzle, and pop;
radiating heat in scorching waves
throughout the air.

By morning only ashes will remain
as evidence of spent passion,
for the stars and the moon
just watch and listen;
Never tell.

Waltz on a Gilded Teapot
By: Barddylbach

    Fur-bell my kitty-cat
oh where would you rather be?
Purr in pristine sunshine
double up the old oak tree.
    Fur-bell my kitty-cat
so where shall we pounce and play?
Over the hilltops prowl
dancing far away;
    Rooftops proudly stretch
as far as the eye can see,
paws and tails on chimney pots
and curly cream for tea.

Gild the teapot, waltz my love!
    Let's bet on what shall be,
beneath that dripping golden sun
    let's dance just you and me.

    Fire-bell king bumblebee
oh where would you rather squeeze?
Buzz in the humdrum sunshine
bustle on the breeze.
    Fire-bell king bumblebee
so where shall we snuggle and sneeze?
Sniffing in humble humming pots
swift and fancy please;
    Queen on guard in her beehive
as far as an ear can tell,
wigs and wags of honeycomb
and flowerpot tea we smell.

Gild the teapot - waltz...

    Fountain-bell blue warrior whale
oh where would you rather be?
Bathe in oyster sunshine
cruise the open sea.

Fountain-bell blue warrior whale
so where shall we snorkel swim?
Deep in the ocean belly
down in the gobbles grim;
   Above the milky wave tops swell
spout over barnacles go,
cockle and sea brew churning
where the broody seaweed grow.

Gild the teapot - waltz...

   Twitter-bell stray swallow
oh where would you rather darn?
Flit under storm cloud sunshine,
nest in that old oak barn.
   Twitter-bell stray swallow
where shallows of the bellbird ring
and echo, there on a rainbow shadow
shall we pitch, fallow and sing;
   In and out of treetops splice
wherever the clade will follow,
over tarn and golden gum entice
in oaksome green sleeves stow.

Gild the teapot - waltz...

   Tusker-bell grand e-le-phant
oh where would you rather stride?
Idle and squat in sunshine,
wat and temple hide.
   Tusker-bell grand e-le-phant
so where shall we cobble and drink?
Brink on the horizon godly plod
abode in the land of pink;
   In tree thugs thicket rub
that trumpet, rump and snout,
plonk and dunk in quango tea
slinking sloppy stout.

Gild the teapot - waltz...

    Thumper-bell tooth tiger lily
oh where would you rather meet?
Hunt in sizzling sunshine,
lord of the jungle beat.
    Thumper-bell tooth tiger lily
so where shall we dine and eat?
Amid the clifftops scowl,
tall and handsome greet;
    Fiercely fearsome growl
beyond those whiskers reach,
tawny toothsome teacup twitch
and awesome prickly peach.

Gild the teapot - waltz...

    Twinkle-bell great silver sea
oh where do I farthest float?
Glisten in bristling sunshine off
the remotest island coast.
    Twinkle-bell great silver sea
so when shall we steal away?
Eternal engines rolling
where night melts into day;
    Over snow clouds star bound
as far as the eye can see,
whims and whams on wattlepot whirls
to pour my silver tea.

Gild the teapot, waltz my love!
    Let's dream of what shall be,
between those solvent silver stars
    let's dance just you and me.

Floral Needs of Waitressing
By: Becky Upchurch

I dug in the dirt today

fingered richly fine loam
that soft organic food for bush, plant
that cup of water for rooting lips
that frangipan hardened clay dessert
on floral tables in my delighted sight.

I was a busboy today

removing remnants, table orts,
lopping clean the once aromatic tops
from the stemmed table legs.
They had signaled to me, their leave.

But where the tip landed was in that fine loam

where roots will play and learn
of the long winter's pause
when in the Spring
I shall waitress for them, again

Weeping Willow.
By: Bellvadear

Weeping Willow.
Why must you cry?
For with every season, changing,
a part of you must die.
One cannot keep blowing around the same leaves,
as you did when you were a younger bark.
Remember when you were the only tree here,
before they built this park?
Life cycles and stages to evolve,
we all must adapt.
For something to grow beautifully,
we must accept that.
We are built to be strong,
and light up this place.
No need to rush things,
swiftly move with grace.
Feel the wild, warm, breeze, on the summer days,
the calm, resting, quite, from winters embrace.
The birds who once nested,
high in your trees,
also move on to raise their own families.
The flowers that die, bloom again next year,
for a brighter shade next time,
fields of rainbows will appear.
All the animals and bugs,
go into a deep stage of sleep,
A time of reflection and balance to keep.
For when they all wake,
a new age they have reached,
a second chance to live,
and learn, and to teach.
Someday when you are just a stump here,
all you have nurtured will flourish, my dear,
all that you created, cared for and loved,
will thrive on long after, your time here is done.
So love while your here,
and have faith for when your gone,
that you did your best,
to help this place carry on!

Lost Soul
By: Ben Meraki

Tear-stained pillow.
Crimson sheets.
A broken heart at rest.
A troubled mind at peace.

Weeping willow,
mighty tree.
No longer bound by your own roots.
Fallen yet free.

As the river takes you on your journey.
The machine that cut you keeps on turning.
We are but single grains in the shifting sands of time.
A flame that burns and fades in the blink of an eye.

I've been waiting for you here.
I'm your protector, have no fear.
My darkness hides you from the demons.
No pain, no anguish. No more reasons to cry those tears.

You lie so still now,
wrapped in velvet sheets.
Photograph clutched to your chest.
Snow-white cheeks.

A smile that never fades.
No furrowed brow.
Those emerald eyes no longer betray you.
All's peaceful now.

Don't grieve for the ones you left behind.
They all will understand in time.
Those who loved you most take comfort that you're free.
Your ever-youthful ghost lives on in memory.

I've been waiting for you here.
I'm your protector, have no fear.
My darkness hides you from the demons.
No pain, no anguish. No more reasons to cry those tears.

Weeping willow,
sacred tree.
No longer bound by your own roots.
Fallen yet free.

Surely Eden Would Look Like This?
By: Bikerfamily

Just a day out, in-between the rain
We took a ride on the half-size
compartmented metal carriage train

Every corner of the park
Took my breath away
The gardens were so beautiful
It made me think of heaven
Surely Eden would look like this?
The colours of the flowers
So divinely shaped, by unseen hand
Perfection or angels kisses left behind
To lovingly inspire the kind

The birds from exotic lands
my Indian hornbill, who danced
energetically upon his branch
having ate his meal

The orange red bird that dived
between the oasis leaves
watched over by the giant sloth
gripping pipes over head

and in the far side corner
my friend, the large fruit bat who slept
supporting his angular wings
without a comfy bed

the wonderful kooky anteater
designed by nature's dramatic hand
evolution and genetic miracle
consuming nutritious food
gifted from the land.

My rhinos, a family of six
who indulged in a deep mud bath
With no shyness, seen in the glory of the moment
It took me to another world, as they played
These giant animals
who could crush with weight
The weather seemed to suit them fine

I wrapped my plastic purple raincoat
To push the cold rain away
I found the wonderful giraffes
With beautiful deep brown eyes
The wooden skywalk put us on a equal footing
As we looked close eye to eye
they munched on clumps of hay
As I reluctantly turned to go
It was definitely a perfect day
in this wildlife garden
and I would have liked to stay.

A Crumpled Composition
By: Blindspot

I am an afterthought,
...a paper dream...
folded and forgotten
in the pocket of your jeans,
A stolen kiss,
lost in your flee
from the sweet store,
The shadowed curve
of a crescent moon,
half of a whole
dangling in sacrifice
to the stars that outshine,
a final teardrop
before the slaughter,
purged into edges
of loves last breath

I am the jagged silence,
of a broken wish,
a jaded blade of nexus
lodged into the soul
of a heart unguarded,
your fingerprints still linger,
fresh upon the handle of promises,
reflections of a smile on loan,
burned into the sword before the slay...

I am the fragmented child,
in search of a voice, that beckons,
whispers are the only map,
I hold on to the edge of them,
illusive tracks of this runaway train,
screaming through the darkness
into the light of your voice
aimless feet, a step ahead
of destiny,
always two steps behind
the crossroads

of that place
where love awaits me...

Petals from my hair,
blow into the passing winds,
stealing your breath
from their fragrance,
fading the velvet colours
into stone,
as they fall beneath
my final parade,
crushed and torn,
mere remnants
left behind in footprints,

...of a paper dream....

Stillness
By: Blue Raven

The stillness of winter
hangs from empty branches
like clusters of dead leaves
heavy with frost,

painted platinum
beneath a pitted moon.

Big night clouds
slide across the sky
without a sound,

thin collections of crystal,
fragile as a baby's breath,
scattered
among the silent stars.

The earth lies dormant,
hushed in slumber,

her nakedness
wrapped in a blanket of fog,
dreaming of April.

And I lie here quietly
with dreams of my own,
listening to the rise and fall
of your breath,

so even and unceasing,
it seems a part
of the silence.

Laurent yvan
Tuesday's Timepieces
&
Fillmyeyes and Laurent with Poetry

Grandpa's Arms
By: Laurent yvan

when she cries I rock her
as gently as a grandpa's arms can
because they have known time
and struggle in measure
and are confident in this small
gesture of love

a soft murmur, a lullaby draws
away the fears
and only a few drops escape
her beautiful sad eyes
"sur le pont D'avignon,
on y danse, on y danse"
french she doesn't understand
but the mind draws it's own
meanings from sounds...

fears recede at last,
and the nightmare is replaced
with the Tale of the Prancing Pony
in stereo dreams and technicolor
a sleeping smile lights up her
copper-framed face
and she presses close
hands gripping my shirt tightly,
then relaxing as Morpheus
tenders his grace

sleep, the great weaver of health
claims her quietly
tucked in, safe, she rests
how can I not sit and rock,
watching her,
joining her dreams of innocence
leaving aside my sandpaper slumbers
for a night

Conkering Love Stripped
By: Brian3357

Our love is bare like autumn remnants shed
or chestnut fruit that peels their shell and spikes
whose velcro skin just stick as fastener strips
with zipper... zip. Like hedgehog balls that curl
with flesh so pale it pricks your prickly lips
that leer. With a creamy mouth that licks my skin
and sucks my ebony sliced tongue that slits.

You kiss our palms that cradle breasts that swell
when disco ball enchants in moonlight beams
that drink in eyes moon shaped that deeply swoon

The fractured light spangles red currant blood
that weeps from tiny pricks that prong our skin
By the pricking of this thumb...punctures lust
that wheeze out a breath in gasps panting hot

As sable rosewood hammered hard in the earth,
we stare at ashen piles and say au revoir.
Like molasses, minutes ooze over the flesh
our lascivious lapses last all night
with sempiternal seconds that stretch southwards.

Dead Weight
By: Brihlmann

Certain hopes
must be shed
and allowed to sink,
before their dead weight
drags us down
to shadowy trenches.

Like the hope
that I will grow
shark skin
that your barbed hooks
cannot pierce,
that it will enfold
and dissolve
the rusty ones
already dangling.

That my wounds
will ever completely close,
and salty currents
cease to sting,
cold ones cease to chill.

That storms will
regain their senses,
and no longer
darken the horizon,
nor churn the seas
till waves
clash in angry battle.

Or that my eyes
will ever adjust
to the dim light
of the murky waters
in which we swim,
and grant me more
than mirror flash moments
of clarity.

Portrait
By: Brihlmann

It was not you,
but my fanciful brushstrokes
on your blank canvas
that I loved.

An abstract portrait,
beautiful in its impossibility,
loved even more
because of it.

But it was stripped from me
by shifting winds,
like a kite
that flew too high
and snapped its string.

It could not
endure the storms,
and crashed to earth
tattered and broken.

I knelt beside it,
gingerly touching
its torn edges,
brimming eyes gazing
at its still vivid colors,
wondering
if it could be
salvaged or sewn,

as you slipped
quietly out the door.

Splendidly Enlightened
By: Buttersoft

Silence envelopes
Trees and butterflies alike
A bell jar
Of muffled desires
Tension
Until it cracks

Electric violence unleashed
Splendidly enlightened
The greatest screen
Those trees and
Butterflies again
Sudden suspense release;
A celestial roar!

Floods follow
Then silence

Untitled 2
By: C. Nastu

Crinkling leaves to walked on ground
The trees bare from Autumn's then.
I long to see the bare turn green,
I'll wait till winters end.

It's been so far from colors,
I've seemed to have lost my touch.
I long to see the spring return,
Enough of winters much.

I slip and slide with shovels sound
The sidewalks filled with sand.
Although I hate this time of year,
The white with winters grand.

Bring back the warmth of summer,
As the sweat falls from my brow.
I hope I make the winter months,
As I long for summers now.

That's How You Look To Me
By: CandyBrown

the soil remembered;

dawn's orange glow,
the days of
horse and plow
sweat upon the brow
winter's chilling snow,
fields ripe of grain
and some not sown,
each time you prayed
for rain, the evenings
you stood alone,
wondering about
another existence
but knowing there was
nothing else you'd
rather do, than this-

even when times
were tough, and you
couldn't get a fair price
for harvested crops
so all the bills
didn't get paid
for another few months
yes (at times)
it was rough,

but
you kept going,
kept working on broken
down equipment,
knowing that planting
season was just ahead,
so you prayed
a little harder,
what was the words
you said?

Dear Lord;
tomorrow is another day
i need you here
beside me
come what may,
bending down
scooping up the soil,
as it sifted through
well worn fingers,
thank you Lord
was whispered,

and the soil
remembered.

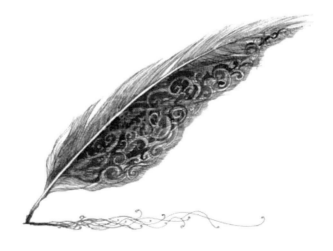

Give a Pulse
By: Casey Haldaine

The shade of light
is set by your presence.

The rain plays drums
on a flickering lamp,
my boots are splashing
to a rhythm.

The drops on the road
and the running engines,
the moons and distant stars,
recreated
in each puddle.

You
give a pulse
to a faceless street

Napalm Memories
By: Cheryl Wilcox

I waited for the fall of Saigon
almost as long
as I waited
for you.

Yesterday gathers
deadwood dreams
and fallen leaves
that whisper your name.

Rusted memories
and destinies
rustle in the wind
and I know
this will always
be our place.

The last kiss
of innocence
touched my lips
that fall of '69

but part of me
still waits for the boy
with the dimpled chin

long after

Napalm and Nixon
carried you home.

Palm Tree Pillows
By: Chinaski

Coffee steam rises
as eyes slowly open
listening to seagulls
as they
languidly glide
above
driftwood ports

Randomly lifted
spirits lost in
BLUE
Dragged
lead feet
made of
planted seeds
tossed
into warm blankets

Sparkling
paths kiss
the infant
sun

Double bass blues
drip off
sandy radios
lost
forgotten
moments
filled with
whispers
Smoky rooms
snapping fingers
dancing into liquid
night

Beach beds
palm tree pillows
among moon
silhouettes
Vacancy signs
painted in
blinking

neon

the station clock stopped in the middle of an one way ticket
By: Constcor

she sat on the trunk in a state...

handkerchief lamenting deflate
sodden in Marmara lake
wringing dry the sea salt intake

locomotive coiled rattlesnake
scorched in a sticky sun cake
where to? another mistake

off the rails in a field of cornflake
lost, re-found, arriving too late
sweet and sour on the same round plate

When I was in love with you
By: Constcor

The flower-power of my garden
has varnished your moon with may-lilies,
dripping them from the heaven of a milky cwm.

Your alit glacial ozone of minimal space
spilled marbled spells
over closed eyes
offered by the craving face
of my flooded glares.

Sizzling,
my palms curved into your perfection,
lacing phosphorescent fingers
round stelar cyclones.

Fresh toes of primordial feet stomped
onto sweet-violet beds,
crisping them in icy dew.

And I treaded the grass blades with lustful soles,
prickled by the frosty bites of the earth.
And I adored you a hundred times till the morning;
giving you the spin of my spine and my waist.

My breast, elevated to your opaline lips,
hanging on your every silvery rustle,
pulsed birdlike
embraced by your wing.

I cast my spell and lived.

Walk Me Through Old Memories
By: CRL17

WALK ME THROUGH OLD MEMORIES...
I sat down at the bar last night
To drink my day away
When a cowboy sat down next to me
And he began to pray.
He said, "Lord, I know I drink too much
But it helps take the pain away.
And Lord my gamblins' out of control,
I lose almost all of my pay."
I turned to him and then I said
Your heart must be full of scars.
This dusty place aint quite a church,
God wont hear you in this bar

Pour me another tall one
Play me another song
Walk me through old memories
Just to help me get along
Pour me another tall one
Another double shot of Jack
Walk me through old memories
Please help me get her back.

He turned his head and then he said
Son, you might be surprised.
God don't care about the why or where
We're all special in his eyes.
I've had my share of heartaches
More than you'll ever know
But the thing that keeps on hurting me
Is the love that I let go.
So I drink too much and I pray each day
But I'm still here all alone
And I walk through my old memories
Hoping someday she'll come home.

Then the bartender came over to me
Sat down two more beers
He said, "It's too bad about that old cowboy
She's been gone for twenty years."

Bigotry...
By: CRL17

BIGOTRY...

When you were a child, ever so small
you lived in a world of your own
In your little world evil didnt exist
No hatred, no suffering, just home

You were so happy, no cares in your life
Playing all the games that children do
Your day consisted of fairy tale people
and sometimes a nap around two.

As the years started going and you started growing
Suddenly the innocent games turned to pain
You found hatred and evil around every corner
Friends started calling you names

Some people decided that you were a target
Just from the color of your skin
You couldnt understand why someone would judge you
They never looked for the love from within

If only the innocence of a child could be given
To those who learned anger and hate
You're only one person, but there's still a chance
To show them its not too late

All you can do is share all your love
Dont let them drag you down
Maybe if you try to think like a child
Someday they may come around.

Magic In The Moonlight
By: CryStan

Magic in the moonlight,
boredom freed
within the flames.

Fearless faces
fill the stadium,
sporting masks
and sharing laughs.

Nightmares long forgotten
as the notes leave
the piano.

Toes tapping,
bodies swaying,
children bouncing in their seats.

A bluejay dives
into the mud,
splashing the freckled face
of a boy
who simply laughs.

He plucks the flower,
"secretly,"
then turns and
gifts it
to the girl.

He tells her
that it must have
grown just for her,
of course.

The tired mom
ascends the staircase
to break up a heated
game of Chess.

A soft breeze shifts
and makes its way
across the open road.

Heads turn with my own,
to inhale the scent
of marshmallows
still roasting
to perfection,

mixed with just a touch
of clean laundry

coming from the window
of the house
with the lady

who stayed indoors

tonight.

Deborahlee
Sizzlin with Sensuality

Fingertips brush...
By: Deborahlee

Flurries of desires rustle deeply,
yearnings edges collide to fill.

Golden leaves of your lips ply
in fragments I recall sweetly.

Arms aching, I am bruised by
memories swept into abyss.

Snowed under by butterflies tickle
intensity of their flutter consumes

Whispers of past scarlet kisses provoke
picture pieces flashing inside my brain

Body longs to connect skin to skin
your embrace haunts my closed eyes

Together wings beating lightly touch
either side of a single wooden door.

Have mapped in branches weave
monochrome touch enveloping.

My skin burns tight awaiting
your sweet enforcement.

Fingertips brush across flesh ablaze
mouth waters, tongue moistens soft lips

Synchronized undulations induce frenzy
breaths pant in tune to pulses melody

Bodies sing songs in lust filled harmony
currents of bliss infuse final contentment

Collaboration with A P Taylor

Briar Patch of Humanity
By: D.Ann

We step in the briar patch of humanity
feeling a few thistles and thorns,
frail hearts sliced with dread
lay bleeding tattered and torn.

We find we're caught in the
thick of these brambles,
our childlike trust
gutted and in shambles.

Harrowing we teeter on the
edge of despair

and behold...

a sunburst alights darkened corners
regret evaporates in thin air!

In the ocean of humankind
tears moisten the crust
of prejudiced lies,
we believe miracles still pulse
and we SHOUT...
transformation arise!

A Voyage Into The Dark
By: D.Ann

Covered in a blanket of melancholy...
strangling in frivolous folly.

Wisps of light sputter then are snuffed out,
salted face peels a discombobulated pout.

Webs of capillaries exposed,
ensnared by the dominance of 'those.'

Coveting shadows... still craving the light,
vibrant heart devoured too weak to fight.

A portrait of a dour expression,
innocence swallowed up in
seething aggression.

Scrutinizing bleeds gritted teeth,
demands are made
to pull out the guts from beneath.

In the cellar of the soul
lurk demons of yesterday's failures,
ideas suffocating yearn for an inhaler.

Weary and bewildered
I'm slammed to my knees,
crawling back into this text
sculpting my own thoughts to appease!

Poets Heart
By: DarkBlueDominion

the purging of a poet's heart
opens up and bleeds for all to see
raw emotions spilled on pages
the soul displayed unselfishly

all the passion all the heartache
inner most feelings shared in word
private depths of one's essence
on exhibit to be felt and heard

it is no simple task to bear
to leave one's self unguarded
throw all caution to the wind
give of self whole hearted

to share the secrets of their life
perhaps create a heartfelt verse
captivate whomever reads
transport, convey, immerse.

-2012/revised 2017-
-Buzz Owen-

Pure Ascension
By: DarkBlueDominion

driven by the pulse of something
hidden deep within the night
ethereal waves wash over me
casts me up in brilliant light

now set aloft my spirit lifted
I'm spun into a realm of soft abyss
rising even faster I float freely
sailing through the silken mist

spiraling into infinite perfection
with fluid motion I am released
within a swirl of unknown colors
I am transfixed in overwhelming peace

now adrift in shimmering currents
soaring through the astral plain
thrust into vast eternal oceans
my pure ascension is attained.

-2012 -
-Buzz Owen-

Space Love
By: Dashpatl

SPACE LOVE — the ejection

"Tower-One we are at Mach-1 and holding."

Transonic gliding
with space-faces smiling.
Yet we hear nothing
suspecting an unconnection
at the speed of sound.

Moody space ice showered the stratosphere.
Petroleum based clouds shimmered with storms.
Sick in quarters together,
each inside a pod
we looked at each other.
Noting simultaneously
our painful passion vacuum
with zero gravitational pull.
Both were equally annoyed by
the space pump sex drive
button blinking : "HYDRO-COOLED".

"We were savages once.
Stuffing our mouths
with unwashed flesh.
Starving for each other.
Our nightly sleeplessness and passionate musings
replaced by temperature controlled meditation
and volunteer work."

The pods entombed us tightly.
Programmed to auto-squeeze.
When I thought I saw reflected
in his mirrored goggles
A terrified lateral gaze.
But papoosed in pre-jettison position,
I could not comfort him.

The calm of space anesthetized our regrets,
which in turn unlocked our belts.
And at a count of zero our pods ejected.
The two of us gently floating acrobatic bodies
accelerating differently,
as we entered the black hole.

A Letter to Santa Claus
By: Dave Proffitt

Dear Santa:
my name is Lindsey
well, I live with my Daddy
Mommy died a few years ago

Daddy said she got real sick
I think he said it was cancer?
I don't know what that means
But I don't have a mother anymore

Daddy doesn't have a wife either you see
Then two weeks ago our old Dog died
He got sick too.
Everyone's getting sick.

Sometimes I see Daddy
when he thinks I don't
and he has tears in his eyes
he works so hard for me

He calls me "Lil' Darlin"
I like the way he says it
He always picks me up
he's so tall

I think Daddy misses Mommy
So Santa I only have one
present I wish you could bring
I wish you would bring Daddy
and me a new wife and Mommy

Sometimes I hear Daddy talking
to Mommy
he says: "Honey you should see Lindsey!"
she looks a lot like you, has your eyes"

"She's getting to be a big girl

"She does real good in school"
We lost "Mr. Doggy" the other day
had to put him down his hips ya know?
Broke Lindsey's heart"

That's what Daddy said to the ceiling
he looks up when he does this
he doesn't know I watch him
Please Santa bring him another wife?"

"I think he might break pretty soon
if you don't?"
I might too.
A new Doggy would be good?"

Please don't put him in the stocking though
It might break?
Thank you Santa, I know I am asking a lot
Lindsey Proffitt

Michelle Held The Butterfly Queen
By: Deborahlee

she wears twin-scepter antennas
circles the hedge leaves of green
dots mark wing edges outlined black
stained-glass lines trace tangerine

on milkweed buffet, she nibbles
dining on the juicy cuisine
sipping periwinkle nectar
from a blossoming canteen

sun tints the skyline cantaloupe
at stops on migration routine
a kaleidoscope flies the horizon
to rendezvous in a ravine

darting, she zigzags an air ballet
two spiraling wing tips careen
reining in a perfumed throne
adds a color pop to the scene

six legs cling as her crew draws close
lands and hails the Thistle Queen

Nature's Beauty
By: Debra Joe

As I stand by the pier I watch nature's beauty

A clear blue sky and the birds flying high in the sky

The river flows ever so softly

As if not to disturb the silence of nature

Stillness and calmness in the air you can feel

For that is the beauty of nature.
So silent sweet and serene.

Summer Past
By: Dod

The last of low light lancing sun
through the August fading leaves
pierced through the serried ranks
of sycamore and grey barked beech
that set alight the trace of vapour
that gathered softly in the dark.

Old elm now gone with sad adieu
so alder, birch, with rowan red,
gnarled youthful oak of twenty years, not more,
bow round the ancient hump backed bridge
a frame for nature's greyed out scene
behind organza struck by morning's beam.

Three kine drop lowing down the bank
their wet and spotted noses low
to crystal current flashing bright
with errant lucis winning through
sharpened bramble tangle sporting fruit
of youthful rose midst guarding thorn.

Rapped still I stand and let the scene
in muted mutters tell of Summer past
gone like that glowing vapour's morn
and bid me dwell on harvest home
for man and land have worked in heat
to store the good for Winter's chill.

Woven Deceit
By: Dragon Sorceress

Woven web black widow spider will weave
Her anger brewing about to combust
For in this player she had placed her trust
Entrapping the hapless that will deceive

His lusty affairs she could not forget
As to his demise she did it with style
mesmerized him with astonishing guile
He showed no remorse or any regret

Donning her cape of deep darkened despair
How many broken hearts did his love kill
With latest betrayal his blood would spill
Took too many lovers for her to care

Her anger brewing still coming in waves
Black widow spider now casting her spell
Alas poor Yorick she knew him too well
This faceless lover there will be no graves

The Dawn of Winter
By: Drunken Monk

November set in as I prepared for an early frost
As, the mercury dipped low and low as the days passed
Covering myself with an woolen overcoat and leather gloves, I treaded down
the street
Lit by the dim oil lamps, and the aura of the moon which was at its peak

The trees started to bare themselves all apart
As, it shed it's green in the gardens and the park
And, the branches became stiff and grey
As, the cold wind blew, and reminded that she has come to stay for long

Flowers shed petals to petals, as if they were cursed by the divine
And, the birds returned to their nests chirping may be about a storm
The, storm which brings in the hail and snow as it rose
Covering the ground with the shiny white, as now no plants grow

Seeing, the plight of the living and the dead as the chill set in,
I, refused to enjoy its beauty and cursed the omnipotent for this sting.
But, O' did this fool realise that he was wrong all along
As, the winter was not an evil eye of the devil, but the divine metamorphosis
of the   nature

The earth sow it's seeds in the cover of the white blanket of the winter
So, that the Eden blooms as the spring evolves
As, winter is the time where the earth strives to toil hard on her barren skin
For, the exhibition of her panoramic beauty once the cold winds stopped and
the easter tide set in.

Panther Creek
By: Edhunter

Early summer morning
a young lad at play

Fascinated by rippling sound
Of water
flowing over rocks, ledges, boulders and clay

Enlightenment of life's source
Leave's him breathless

Mesmerized by energy and power
Courage is taken at his very best

Aqua pura is to his knees

Chill is overthrown by excitement and laughter
Jumping; dancing and playing
Not knowing the mud his clothes are after

This is the best time of his life

Until he gets home

From the soil on his clothes
That's when his mother will know

He spent the day at Panther creek

Loving You
By: Edward Torres

Holding your soft hand
barefoot walking on the sand
watching the boardwalk lights
brisk air blows these October nights
lost in your eyes
as they put the ocean to shame
hair falling
off those shoulders
pink bikini top
and cutoff jeans

smiling and laughing
sitting on the shore
cold waves splashing
warm lips kissing
watching
silhouettes
of birds flying
in the sunset sky
arm around you
head on my chest
fingers tracing
tattoos

salty air
sea breezes
making
the palm trees dance
nature and weather
making a perfect scene

candle lit dinner
bouquet
yellow, pink, and red roses
drinking
coconuts and wine
brush my thumb

against your blush cheeks
you bite your lip
smirking
while I nibble
your neck
everything I do
is because I can't,
stop loving you

I am that I am
By: Eric Svenson

Arrested here I dwell
sculpted iceberg curve and cavern my solace
Aquamarine lighting romancing the endearing moon
dreams of cavorting polar bear cubs stream

Arrested here I'm compelled
expelled to sing praises with angelic realms
Evergreen heart chambers embrace dark orchestral manouvres
leap and skip with swift salmon effervescence into the Light

Arrested here I daily genuflect
flow with wild horse manes streaming through snow
Knave and architrave sculpted by ice
natural cathedrals cloistering nature's bounty

Arrested here I accept
the equanimity of my cleansed soul
Peat and moss secure, my healing heart endures
whale bone bleached white, pure and pristine

'Hark! Lend me thine eager ear
for God so loved the earth and the fullness thereof
That He set aside the crystalline fields of Iceland
where tracts of volcanic ash whisper perpetual pardon

All things bright and beautiful
All things wise and wonderful
Set aside in my secret garden of Iceland
Love arrested me here where Seraphim still stand guard

Gateway - wormhole - funnel
tunnel of exalted throne room where energy rests
Confluence of shifting - sighing snowdrifts concur
waltzing Northern Lights perpetually praise heaven's stairway

Beyond Harbours of Doubt
By: Essama Chiba

Travelling light
unburdened by baggage
that weighed down the spirit

Most come with nothing
created from clay
like that of pottery

Heading to their destiny
sailing oceans of agony
leaving behind harbours of doubt

Pearls and coral emerge
from the depth of sadness
waves elevated in the sea
like mountains

The earth will perish
flooded with tears
and there will remain
only your face

Pam Ray
Into The Darkness
&
Share The Laughter

We Are Defined Together
By: Pam Ray

we are defined together
here in this moment
where palm reads palm
and life touches life

becoming thoughts
entwined
becoming one

I love you
because I know you

I know you
because the heavens
introduced us
before we spoke a single word
to each other,

even in the silence
of our somber hours
the moon smiles wistfully
to grasp that exchange
between two hearts
which cannot be completely understood
but simply felt

if the breaths we nourish
here on earth
are the rise and fall of the morning glory
and we learn the frailty
of our own humanity

we will still find strength in love,

when your bones cross my bones
and our lips no longer touch as flesh
our souls will grow ivy rings
around garnet towers

even if the physical testimony
of who I am changes
you will still know me

by the geranium I place in your hand.

Burnished Dawn
By: Eveningstar

Dawn comes quickly,
in burnished streams of rose
and blue, to banish the
shadows of the city's alleys

That wander in cobbled rivers,
with waterfalls of steps leading
you into leftover pools of light,
shyly hiding from the sun

Coaxing shade from ivy,
roses yet slumber before
their petals warm
into a teasing release
of scent

To be carried into open
windows, while the houses
stir and shake off the night,

To greet the dawn

...There I Meet The Black Panther
By: Ezekiel9940

Running barefooted
surrounded by teasing darkness
moonlight caress
Dried foliage are feathers
along the ancient road I trek

An unfamiliar scene
conjured in a dreamy masquerade
under the myriads of dryads and nymphs
Spellbound and tumbling
in an emerald paradise

Towards the verdant curtain
a regal presence stood in my path;
flesh clothed in shadow silk
no thrones of gold and stones
no crowns that stood in its fierce brow

Savagery entangled
in the vines of otherworldly beauty
While both death and life
are the scepter and globe
it held under its paw

Bearing the eyes
of saint and beast
I cower in the amalgam
of fear and bliss
As he approach with silent steps
that it deafens the cosmos itself

Will he pass the law of the jungle?
To me who is but a humble wanderer
a sole trespasser
enthralled adventurer

Or will it bless me
by its moonlit fang
sharpened by myriads
of secrets
only sang by primeval voices?

Like a knight in the presence of his king
my knees bend to received
The teeth of his majesty
Then it all comes back to me
That I was devoured by wisdom itself

Photographer
By: Fillmyeyes

Through His Eyes
I see the wonder of the sunsets.
the beauty of God's painted skies
I see the perfection
of huge rocks
against the backdrop
of simple brush
and clouds

I see the uniqueness of
others around me
the beauty of their
individuality
captured
on their faces

I see the hidden calm
captured in photograph
of the single tree
standing quietly
as if in
prayer

the world appears bigger
brighter and much
more colorful
than my recollection
from the time before
he entered into my life

Through his eyes
I have seen myself
the strength
of my convictions
the depth
of my devotion
the power
of my will

and the beauty
of my gift

Through your eyes
I see eternity

Silver Sorrows
By: Gemme Scribe

As mellow mornings adorn the pristine white skies
Where the prism of your wilted sun slowly fades
Into the silhouette of your blackened memoirs
Haunting me in the shadows brought by our tainted yesterdays
Living with the burning rays of your scarlet infused sins.

Where the dusky sunset strums to the melody
Of your shaded agonies which brought an empty embrace engraving the lost
lullabies
I began to sing with the silver sorrows lurking in my twilight heart
For in the whispers I hear within every beat
Is the lighthouse I began to follow in the wilderness
Of this blossoming nightfall.

In the soft whimpering echo of this tranquil midnight
You were the promised star to burn in the satin skies
Of my nocturnal galaxies as you paint the crystal embers
With the charcoal dreams in blushing glow of the moonlight
Waltzing to the flicker of your dying flames as these cold tears rain the
loneliness
Of my mascara eyes.

Underground
By: GeorgiSilentPoet

Flowers withdraw
underground
Their scent snuffed out
by Autumn winds

Sleeping to the hum
of tube trains whooshing
through twilight London
buried deep

Kissed by Spring
and arranged to order,
they'll proudly glide down
pew-lined aisles

or personalised and
artistically sculptured,
be laid with reverence
on scented graves

In order to write - she plays miss faithful
By: Gill Blaze

marianne that is;
her husk draws a long drag
on a cigarillo; in her honour
she would buy a tin
of café cremes
a slow smoke of history
& time goes by

just the stroke of sulphur
makes her think
of how a certain song
triggers her into a semi-conscious daze
flares of smokerings puff
through the minus temperatures

sifting through memorabilia
the stones live at maine road
manchester
when her and the 'big fella'
were happily embraced under
a bright manchester skyline

now: as time has flown away
with mr & mrs magpie
and marianne is no longer
the apple to mick's eye
or as the big fella always said:
bring it michael thomas!

she reclines in the new chair
new back
support
& she 'sits and watches as tears go by'

not for a sadness
but joy
not for loss
but love

now she understands why marianne
still smokes a lovely song

Bathing Sublime
By: Greyeyes Smith

Darkness, whispers into itself,
like ears of dog, on life's bookshelf.
Delighting senses, not known to man,
further the Creators, sacred plan.

Shivered ripples, echoing time,
through oceans of space.
Waves, bathing sublime,
grooves record, soulful retrace.

Fingers follow lines, upon the old ones faces.
Cosmic breezes, mingled last breaths.
No sever, wrought, as we lived our deaths.
Races and places,
names changed, but, never the faces.

From a twinkle, within our eyes.
Old souls peering out, seeking ancient, reprise.
Cliff tops, hold her spirit there,
lonely she waits for her sailor fair.

Never taken, only torn, she outlived her captors and their evil glare.
To lay with her husband in a realm out there.

Open armed, he beheld, her child inside,
gently repairing the tears of his bride.
Eons they danced in fevered romance,
every atom of water, holds their song,
carried on breezes, sweet and strong.
Rebirthed, wanton love at every chance.
Some of the paths were winding and long.

Onward, they fought as they harbored their love.
Now it's all around them, eagles and falcons, carry their feathered entwinment,
on high above.

Wolves skulk in the mist,
guarding from attack with fierce desist.
The story I tell you is hallowed, it's true, for their, essence of knowing, resides
inside you.

The Old Barn
By: Greyeyes Smith

The heifers were utterly shocked
Startled as the chickens flocked
And the lonely bull balked
Goats gathered and whisper talked
About the farmer and the weed he stocked
And all the cookies he ate,
From the cupboard he kept locked, and the milk he drank as the wind socked.

Comfortably Numb
By: Gwendolyn Brown

Comfortably Numb
A slight smile curves dry cracked lips
his head vibrates as colors swirl
around his brain

a beautiful kaleidoscope of patterns

He catches gigantic lemon drops
from the sky
sweet and tart, it's all coming together

he feels nothing, yet he feels it all
in his world he is an over comer

he's on cloud nine...

Eyes a dirty blue rolling around like marbles in their sockets
sweat drips from greasy limp hair

He sits on a scarred up bathroom floor
leaning against a dingy graffitied wall

a rubber band still around his arm
an empty syringe next to him
sirens in the air...

as he gets comfortably numb
A slight smile curves dry cracked lips
his head vibrates as colors swirl
around his brain

a beautiful kaleidoscope of patterns

He catches gigantic lemon drops
from the sky
sweet and tart, it's all coming together

he feels nothing, yet he feels it all

in his world he is an over comer

he's on cloud nine...

Eyes a dirty blue rolling around like marbles in their sockets
sweat drips from greasy limp hair

He sits on a scarred up bathroom floor
leaning against a dingy graffitied wall

a rubber band still around his arm
an empty syringe next to him
sirens in the air...

as he gets comfortably numb

Questions
By: Haunted Memories

If I offer a drink
From my cup of misery
Will it quench your thirst

If I offer a view
Into my haunted soul
Would your curiosity be satisfied

If I was an open book
Word by word page by page
Would you be but a chapter

If I put my heart in your hand
Full of holes and scars
Could you find its beauty

If I returned to dirt
Ashes free in the wind
Will there be tears

Haunted Love
By: Haunted Memories

Dripping..........

My love is slowly leaving your heart,
Brighter days now lay lost in the dark.
Replaced by a new emotion growing wild,
Staying strong as you left I only smiled.

Flowing............

Random thoughts of heart verses mind,
Knowing it must be true that love is blind.
I can't see another left only with visions of you,
For me this love is real, pure, honest and true.

Longing..........

To look into the depths of your eyes,
Praying it's a nightmare instead of goodbye.
One touch; one last kiss before you go,
Forever empty as you have reaped my soul.

Alone..........

Shadows on the wall my only company,
Together haunting me in perfect harmony.
As the sun sets and the day fades,
Saltwater in my eyes calls your name.

Natures Clarity
BY: HELIOTROPE WINE

Reaching out and truly changing
Grasping trying and trying is gaining.
To sit in stride. To do nothing
Outside.
An entire world waits to be explored.
Technology's advances keep u in a hoard.
It's nature that people are truly missing.
Where waterfalls play and dance upon the creek.
Take pride to watch its perpetual flow.
And hear the waters liquid know.
Where if dull eyes from city sky's for an instant
Can get away. In natures depth to gaze upon
The healing intensity of the waterfall's way.
It's harmony remains consistent. Its flow it
Stays the same.

IntimidusRex
Into The Darkness
&
Share The Laughter

Menisperma and stardust (for angeleyez)
By: IntimidusRex

Take my hand! Tis a sojourn we embark.
Those blest shards of light and laughter debate
Color'd aural blooms, that grow with a spark
'Pon meadow'd impressions, where warmth doth wait;
Sleep and dream in menisperma's embrace
Walk on jade glens, midst that soft summer cress
While poltergeist breezes, never grieve, their place
And eyez flutter to, angel'd wings caress-
Stardust fireflies brighten those paths, alone
As nature's sussurance willst calm thy sowl,
Breathe deep, ambrosia's honeysuckle cologne
Filling your wings as we sit on that knoll,
Tis time! Sweet angel, tis time! To arise
Where wonders never cease, e'en butterflies

To the gentle hymn of heaven
By: Hippy Adam

And only sometimes
Would i breathe with angels
Who move suns and dead flowers
To hastened winds of wings
That long for the moon---

I am one day too soon
To realize the barriers of death
Cannot be raised to love and loss.

I have slept with gods who bury
Their floral shade for sunrise,
Not knowing that now,
Somewhere
Beneath the stars
And flowers you held
For odes of want and need,
For love will sprout
To the pedestal
As all things in secret
Are meant to be buried---

Ah, this sun of sunset
And rise of sunrise
Will ripple to the grove,

Remembering the softest rain
And mid-spring clouds of heaven
Tilting to angelic streams
That pour onto her lips

And the sky is nigh,
Night to kissed rain
To our tempest fade,
Ah, love, to you.

Nature's beat
By: Huesfac3

The sounds of rapid down pour
On rusty, hazy zinc roof sheets
In harmony with the soft groans
From heavy dark clouded canopy;
Soft flashes tweet and squeal
Melodies of distant hope of surplus.

Towards the city's hall overflow,
A conglomerate of choral singers
With croaks and stridulations;
Night at alert on alarmist's screeches,
Fill dark pond's waters with jingles;
From bongo vibes, the music flows.

Pining inside out of silhouette trees,
Sagging, tapping with flute and hoots;
From a distant mountain, the alpha
Calls out at full moon; forest sheds
Leaves and furs to unknown destinations;
A coarse undertone—the loiterer's sigh!

White dove submerges sunrise,
The deadened forest perforated
By scintillating sunrays; eyes twitch,
Awakening mellow, sweet sounds
Of morning songbirds in eden;
All sounds harmonise with nature's beat.

Summertime Daze
By: Ice Brat

Please, patch me a lacy spiderweb of daises,
carpeted on a dew-bed of luscious infant blades,
sweetly appease us and flow in deep lavender blown kisses

I grasp ears to hear candy coated giggles from river-sided babies,
as crazed waves crash into multi-colored creations,
which tumble dainty across squealing puckish tickle toes,
warm breathes magnetize from lemonade mouth of angels

play me a hypnotizing little ballad thrummed by bronzed fingers,
play me with a memorizing whistle up and down bikini bottoms,
play me alongside the turquoise river's trek of tree-lined breaches

I reach into my deepest memories of honey-tasting summer gazes,
and trek a little back each time frozen tundra wasteland dazes

Nursery Crimes
By: Iff Ur Abs

Steve saw
Marjorie's jaw
and delighted in
her poetry raw.
Her nursery rhyme
was out of time
so he put in
a hickory-dickory
clock.

The mouse ran up
he'd heard enough
of Aesop's fabled
funny stuff.
he plugged his ears
with cotton balls
and started rapping
with Biggie Smalls

formed 2 Mice Crew
and rap was spewed
but forgot to view
the trap or two
which snapped off
the meece's foot
so the group broke up
they were kaput.

Alison wondered
where to stand
after 2 Mice Crew
broke up the band.
so instead of looking
through the glass
she started to run
down through the pass
over the river
and through the brook

she chased the rabbit
until it shook.
Alice had an Uzi
was on a mission
her stance had taken
a different position.

She shot her way
through Chicago alone
erasing the mem'ry
of Al Capone.
She stopped at Uno
for a slice of deep dish
and fell through a portal
she'd gotten her wish.

She climbed out to
the Jersey Turnpike
and quickly met up
with Our Gang and Spike.
They came over
sat down beside her
calmed her down
with a bitsy spider.

They watched her weave
her little web
when Alison said
it's time for bed.
Darla left the scene
whisked off in a car
so Alfalfa and Spanky
went back to the bar
and hung out there
with Jack and Jill
who had just returned
from over the hill.
Jack's broken crown
bought them all a beer
and they all were happy...
or so it appeared

Red Death
By: Iff Ur Abs

A fly died in my red wine,
I nearly gulped him down,
but I swirled him gently on my tongue
and then I pulled him out.

Once I recognized him
as the insect he resembled,
I over analyzed the thoughts
my prideful mind assembled.

He lingered on my palate,
earthy flavor with full body.
and when I say this wine had legs,
I'm not trying to be snobby.

The wine was aged in west coast oak,
so this guy died with class.
even though his butt got soaked
and he had his funeral in my trash.

So to all beware, a lesson's there
that connoisseurs should not diminish;
don't gulp, savor,
the bouquet and flavor,
or you may miss the complex finish.

poetry... a mysterious esse
By: Indian Girl

poetry isn't written on paper
it flies
...beyond
metaphors and rhyme
stars and life
time and miles

poetry is in a
mother's hopeful labour
newborn's first cry
child's sweet yawn
father's loving scoldings
sibling's playful pranks
all the first days' fears

and more...

a smile through tears
calm shining rivers
waterfalls breaking rocks
raging seas
sunny days
moonlit skies
flying birds
cherished quotes
passion of hearts
music of souls

but,
not just that...

crow's coarse caws
rose's thorns
dried out pen's nib
dull joke's awkwardness
beggar's eyes
scarred face's black past
failed dreamer's curse

drunk's rant
rogue's shattered heart
slit wrist's oozing blood
dying person's last wish
tomb's wilted flowers

forbye...

the first kiss
last touch
fresh vows
broken promises
feelings
detachment
thoughts
lunacy
freedom
abandonment
ice
fire
new beginnings
ever-changin' ends
numbers and science

withal...

cloudy days
dark nights
funerals
forgotten memories
tattered letters
ashes

why only
a lover's ballad?
nature's serenity?
words?

poetry is
me
you
him

her
it
unknown
all who ever crossed ways
also the ones who are evermore still

poetry is a floret that buds in barren icicle
sings when all voices are hushed
outreaches dialects and sunrays

poetry is everywhere
poetry doesn't exist

poetry never dies
poetry was never born

poetry just is...

Life Under A Red Maple
By: Irene Clasper

Under a beautiful 'Red Maple',
a red carpet of red leaves
a worthy occupier of which I am
with my heart so young
singing tunes of love and peace

A worthy hand's work this;
a solace to humans and animals alike,
the whole place with its charm
throbbing vibrantly;
a place where leisure dwells in leisure

I always got lost on my way to November
By: IntimidusRex

you were a fresh margarita (salt-n-sass)

liquid diamonds sought refuge
in the sprocket of your stare,
fingers disentangling Spanish moss curls
caressing swanned grace, dipping to a low cut
summer frock bending time's curved reality,
black-hole's event horizon nipping my heels

I wore a frozen smile

jelly shot implosions
rattled my rickety gait
leaving my feet in Frisco's bay, I
walked on bloody stumps 'neath Alcatraz's eddy

you wore the moon in April showers

May breathed sighs and bikini roses
blushed your soft silk in cherry parfait
embraces, summer's spoon fed glimpses
were lesser desserts, I never understood why-

I always got lost on my way to November
Prompt:
you're the kind of love that taints hearts and
breaks bones. the kind that echoes
uncertainty, and mourns poetry
concurrently. the kind that is conceived in a
breath and decays in the next. the kind that
leaves your body like a bullet, and scars
your skin like a serrated knife- the kind you
start forgetting before it is gone, but live with
long after your chest has succumbed to
gravity.

Waiting
By: JaboUK

She's waiting for the mailman
(oh please don't pass on by)
her love is fighting in the war
she knows that he could die.

He's away in foreign lands,
been gone for two years now,
she's worried but she's coping
at times she wonders how.

She waits there for a letter
as that would ease her pain,
she would know he's still alive
and may see her again.

With dread she sees the young boy,
in fear she holds her breath,
he brings those yellow telegrams
with news of hurt and death.

Her heart is thumping wildly
(oh please please pass on by)
she's so relieved he doesn't knock
she breathes out with a sigh.

Thus she sits and waits and hopes,
when will her anguish end?
if her love should not return
she knows her heart won't mend

A Lame Girl's Lament
By: JaboUK

I wish there was someone who loved me,
someone with whom I could share,
someone to laugh and to cry with,
someone to stand by my chair.

I wish I had someone to love me,
someone so kind who would care,
someone who'd look for the real me,
someone who'd see past my chair.

I wish I loved someone who loved me,
someone to bring me good cheer,
someone to whom I'd seem normal,
someone to hold me so dear.

I wish I had someone to hold me,
I hate to be so alone,
I wish I had someone to cherish,
someone who'd make me their own.

I wish there was someone who loved me,
someone who wouldn't just stare
at my limbs bent and contorted,
surely there's someone - somewhere?

My Cup is Full
By: Kay Crown

Eyes that roam
over endless plains
of golden treasures,
the beauty of a heart
open to its blessings.

There is comfort
in contemplating
the richness of life,
the whirring of wings,
the low buzzing of
joyous satisfaction.

My mind spins through
decades, hovers over
intricate layers of
memories, gliding in
gratitude for rolling
abundance that has
no bounds.

Fillmyeyes

Fillmyeyes and Laurent with Poetry

Touched...
By: Fillmyeyes

Spirit touching spirit....
a simple flutter upon my heart
unlocked the chains
that once bound it.
I let you in...
I allowed you
to touch my life,
to cradle me within
your wisdom,
as well as your peace.
I was yours to love,
if only for a moment
in the realm of an eternity.
I died and was reborn
within your arms.
With your every kiss,
I found myself.
I have lain
naked at your feet,
waiting for the gifts
that spill forth from you,
to flow freely down upon my flesh.
~

I have knelt still upon the grains,
asking silently for tender mercies.
~

Thankful for all He has given.
Touched by His hand upon my head,
upon my heart, and again upon my soul.
Guiding me,
toward a deeper understanding.
Granting me, His peace,
His love, His wisdom
Sheltering my soul patiently
and without question.
Unconditional love.
Sacred beauty,
in the silence,
captured now
within my soul.

Song of the Troubadour
By: Kimberley Baker

Dawn's sunbeams pierce through
the forests leafy canopies.
Blazing stripes to the ground,
illuminating life within the trees.

A natural sanctuary hidden away,
from man's incessant turmoil.
Where you can still breathe the air
and there's no poison in the soil.

No buildings or billboard signs,
to obstruct the amazing view.
No city lights hindering the sight
between the stars and you.

A place where the animals can roam
Without fences they wildly play
Jumping, singing, running and swinging
Freely they live every day.

A place that can only be heard of
in our modern day folklore.
Or in the notes being sung by one
of nature's feathery troubadour.

Hello
By: King isme

Our song came on "Hello" and I broke down into tears
Memories came flooding back at me
Heard almost to the day we started our journey together
It still remains to be at the top of my list

Memories of a past that was hurtful
Pain that I caused you can back to haunt me
Not wanting you to be right always, for you to make a mistake
Perfection was not my game, not like you

Hello, how are you, I hope you're well
I'm sorry for all the pain I've caused you
I wanted to have your acceptance, to not make mistakes
I went about it the wrong way, the past lingers to this day

Giving in, I started listening to you
I started to see what you were talking about
Fear came over me for a short while, fear of getting you hurt
But following your words, I started to change

Changes came about me, scared, I started to run away from you
I ran away from all that was good, all the love you shared with me
Many times I thought of not coming back, of leaving you
But something told me to return to you, that it would be worth it

I never wanted to hurt you, to abandon you like all the rest
I was selfish, now I can see that, that you were right all along
You told me what was going to happen, I wish I could remember
I wasn't truly listening, I was staring at your gorgeous face

Hello, how are you, I'm glad I decided to listen to your wise words
I'm good now, I now am your wife, and so much in love with you
I wait by the phone, hopeful it will ring
When it does, I'll be ready, I'll be the first to say "Hello"

I love you my husband, I miss you more than anything
I never thought I would have to spend so much time apart from you
It's killing me inside, I have to be brave, stay strong for us
But my heart is in pieces, has been since you walked out that door

I hope you return soon, return to be at my side
I love you, miss you, crave to say hi and talk for hours
For now, I write, it's the only thing I know how to do
You taught me, guiding me to be the best, yet to be revealed

I will make you proud of me, you will be proud of your wife
At your side I stay, doing what I do best to get you home
Words are powerful, you taught me that, now is the time to use them
I use my voice to get your story out, for the world to hear

I've got some plans already being finalized, some are just ideas yet
Many things I need to complete, to get you home to your family
Both Kaycie and I are waiting patiently for you
We love you, just the way you are, don't ever change
Within hours, I'll be able to say "Hello", I'm not going anywhere

Little Bird
By: Ksparrow

I found a little bird who'd died
upon the walkway, just outside.
He lay there, very stiff and still,
with empty eyes and silent bill.
I crouched beside him, wondering,
and heard a distant thundering—
a dull salute to little bird,
a rumbling grief, a final word.

And as the drops began to fall
and splash against the garden wall
I gathered up the tiny soul
and took him to a shaded knoll.
I buried him beneath the tree
where once he sang, alive and free,
then stood and walked back in the rain,
reflecting about joy and pain.

I can't explain the tears I shed,
what anguished thoughts remained unsaid—
but something soft inside me stirred
with sorrow for a little bird.

Salty Sound
By: Kym Harrison

Silence bears a salty sound,
ear pressed firmly to the ground,
just to see if life teems there,
beneath this bitter, stagnant air.

No TV, music, people chatter,
children's footsteps, for that matter.
No doors creaking, slamming shut,
no hustle in this daily rut.

No clack or clank upon the stove.
No clippers clipping in the grove.
No clanging box of welcome mail,
or footsteps light upon the trail.

No knock upon my welcome door,
no one to greet me and adore.
No laughter in these empty halls,
no one to hear my desperate calls.

Silence bears a salty sound,
I lay my ear upon the ground.
I listen closely, plead and crave,
with salty tears upon your grave.

Every Emotion Thereof
By: Lady A

Should my words kiss you,
piquant lips brush mine.
sting my tongue,
sensually divine.

Should my eyes write verse,
my rhyme, a composition,
a fusion of your imagery,
and my alliteration.

Should our hands be cotton,
we caress our love.
stir harmony, stir passion,
and every emotion thereof.

You are eternity,
three hundred full moons.
my death brings joy,
to spend infinity with you.

Sacrosanct Sands
By: LaraL11

Out there,
apologies are absent.

Air, unforgiving and piquant -
stealing saliva from my swallows.

Out there,
I learned -
through blister and burn,
lessons from its acrid temper.

Sage shrubs scrubbing
past's rapine stains and
bearing my blames.

Out there,
I would be birthed and
baptized in Basin dust.

On holy clay,
I'd lay and pray to
dusk's purpled mountains -
for they were more immense
than God.

Out there,
crickets croaked
for my
calloused corpus -

With them
I sung from flicking lizard tongue
of the
drydrydry;

free from moisture's lies.

High Desert,
witness to my
emancipated screams -

I've been told they still echo;
held for
the next numb one
who needs to sting
to feel
something.

The Wishing Well
By: Laughingpoet

Some sap (me) wished for true love instead of instead of...
Well, now truly the love has gone and she left me for her true love.
Well...
A deep subject
I wish I wish I wish I wish.

Some sap (her) wished for wealth instead of instead of...
Well, now she's got all my cash, my car, my house, my nest egg, even my goldfish.
Well...
A deep subject
I wish I wish I wish I wish

Some sap (her again) wished for happiness instead of instead of...
Well, now she married her lawyer and they are happy happy with all my cash and my car and my house etc.
Well...
A deep subject
I wish I wish I wish I wish

Some saps (my former wife and her new hubby, her lawyer) stood above that well and wished for peace instead of instead of...
Well, their rotten behinds fell ninety-seven feet to the bottom of that well.
Rest in Peace
Well, anyway,
I finally got my wish.

The Perfect Night
By: Laura Hughes

Sitting on the white sands.
Staring into the sky.
A cold drink in my hands,
and the wind blowing by.

The beauty of the moon,
shining down on the waves.
Nature playing it's tune,
and wonderfully saves.

My soul seems to be soothed,
by the beautiful sounds.
Like the white sand is smoothed,
as the water rebounds.

The stars twinkling bright,
like diamonds in the sky.
Creates the perfect sight,
when the view hits your eye.

That night was perfection,
with no worries or fears.
Sitting in reflection,
the beauty could cause tears.

Under The Paris Blue
By: Laurent yvan

walking down cobbled boulevards
the blue Paris sun is an electric
moment, hanging close to the
soldier trees that stretch green
in rows

worshipful and yearning
they raise frozen arms
leaves drinking from the mother
offering shade to peasant and king alike
in egalitarian equipoise

the city is a mixture of aromas
that come and go on vagrant breezes
repelling or dazzling, scents transport
stealing free will
guiding feet in quickening march

bread of the morning is an
angels breath that kisses me intimately
with its crackling crust and
redolence of creamery butter
seeking marriage with cafe au lait

I am the priest that unites,
the bond-creator that will
never be sundered from his flock
Le Grenier à Pain is my church
where I kneel in daily worship

this heaven on earth steals
all direction and purpose
sidewalk table seated, I partake
in gustatory obeisance under
trees that rustle in familiar hosanna

green
and vibrant
under the Paris blue

Let It Snow Let It Snow

By: Lawrence Fitzger

Wintertime love is wow

Eyes, I can't see

lashes flash there's a

patterned of lace, as snowflakes

melt soft across my lips

exquisite blooms of winter

coldest icy snow shall not freeze

nor will night ever slow or blacken

in the howling, we watch grey skies sway

laugh at wicked, whipping rains

hear only the call

of our names

Faery Hollow
By: Luke Elven

Faeries awaken under
leaven blankets
When spring has dressed
herself
from winters naked exhibition
She will come again

With a fluttering and spluttering
Winged cities emerge
from tulip cocoons
Opening in bloom

In faery hutts they abide
Hidden in hollow's
Of little mushroom hills
A flash of golden leaf
Accorn fashion hats
Wings like butterflies

Peaking through the hollow
Enchanted as a child's eye
As tall as flowers
The racing of snails has began
Whom will win?

For many a child's wishes
Blown on forget-me-nots...
Helicopted down by the roots
Faeries carry there wishes
hanging on till there feet
touch the ground

Childrens eyes would grow
like sunflowers do
If only they knew
where to look...
and not in fairytale books

but the secret places
under window sills
that look out to country meadows

And...if they happened to peep
they would smile and see...
In bluebell pods little people
wait for bumblebee rides
Waving as they fly
To those waving to them-by and by

Smear Their Fog
By: Luyu Wild Dove

This Soul is White Wolf

Bust through the seams, it ain't what it means.
don't strap yourself to someone's ego.
It depends what they are looking for, style, rhyme or be it spiritual karma.

so your a underdog, trying to smear their fog.
i pen for me, for what I see, even things that are obscene. See, them words
that bleed are mine, a picture of the walls..... I push back.

I don't need to change, I don't need to hack your ego shit. Rising from the
spiting flames, I learnt your stupid ass games.

I can freeze up, take my pen and bleed these simple frames. So some see my
name, or my changing colors your, spill'in racism, but, I call the night birds, they
sing the darkness of the words you hid.

my lust, my lyrics give my soul and rush my blood.
the drums of my brothers I celebrate
I bleed dark red and paint my lips that'll make you beg

put them chains, clamp and shackle, you ain't got nothin to loose, try'in and
doing all the same thing, over and over again. Black ink flows, Black ink flows
and puddles below.

Welcome Rain
By: M.K. Rock

valley torrents wash clean this day
hawk cries fracture blackened skies
the clouds expel excessive weight
as sponges wrung in a silken splash
deluge splays o'er cracked clay below

cannon barrage on concussive rails
fire echoes to reverberate through us
sonic drums pummel noon-day depths
reflections pool inside the sun's hide
cowering from nature's arsenal

sky exclaim sears ions afloat
potency wafts of burnt ends strewn,
readied fields grow to future's yield
amber gold trails hold care-tended seeds
seas that soak us with bounty

resurgence urges prompting whips
stark proclaim invites as some dares do
silver flashed splitting darkest hold
lightning snaps bold

elements play
stormy days are often essential norms

A P Taylor

It Goes A Little Bit Like This...

Father To Son
By: A P Taylor

I

Pebbles on the paths,
black gates with crest.
Kings estate, on an
English eve, dark, sallow.
Hunger baying, he stole in
with his father seeking a buck.
Guards with swords patrolled.

On them, right behind,
he dropped his leather swag
and off scattered to flight.
With a buckled belt he was
whipped, the kerosene
lamp glowed, brown on
welts, deep to bone,
an ivory glow.

II

Uneven track wound
back from night shift
at the butter factory.
Fog of a Gippsland morn,
quietly waiting. Writing
to mother country, drunk.
Pen trailed off curled paper.

Placed out his hand
for his pay check.
When it was missing two
pound, he chased
after. Rounding on
him with glancing blows,
bruising, in the pale
light of morn.

III

Footpath sparkled as a
car had blasted into the
glass shop window
to rob the place. More
smashed then taken,
among shards, the boys
ruby lustre bowl.

"Is all the money paid back?"
eldest son asked, looking at
steel shutters, once a
glass and porcelain display.
His anger brewed, he knew the
pay out might cover half.
But he just hugged his son
in the gold of sunrise.

IV

Gates emptied together
as hundreds sought
luggage, among the stone
gardens, metal turntables.
Announcement called him,
to "lost luggage", he trudged
down to a barred window.

Eldest's fencing kit badly
crunched, several foils
broken. Shaking his head
as filled in British Airways claim.
"Flights turbulence", muttered,
while his angry son flapped.
Secured tape, so the leaping deer
image once again zipped closed.

Lost Reflection
By: Mahesh Shroff

Thunder whispers in my ears, moaning
'Have you seen the moon?'
River-dancing in a circle
My fears force me to face the wolves.

Glistening water runs in loops
Sifting sandbanks, shifting views
Watch my dreams come alive
As I try to tear these walls down.

I build a house and call it home
I learned to swim, I have a boat
I wish for faith, I wait for safe
I close my eyes and curse my fate.

Woods Scene
By: Manchilld99

and she pitched haltingly,
stumbling amid the undergrowth,
her tears drying quickly in the chilly fall wind.
an asymmetrical trail of doddering footprints,
snot, urine, and blood foretold her demise.
the doe buckled now, spine snapped, bewildered,
failing at motherhood, gasping for breath, losing life.
ears pert, her spotted fawn watched,
fearfully, knowingly, and stayed back.
beyond the dense thicket, rethinking his ammo,
cursing his rifle, examining again its scope,
an unknowing novice damned his best luck yet.

The Lady In The Red Coat
By: Mark Moir

I told the lady in the red coat my secrets;
they sought refuge in the edges of her smile
and can be seen sleeping in the crinkles of her nose.

They wept all their tears in the cracks of her lips;
and now wait in the shadows of her beauty,
like winter birds perched toward the sun.

My secrets can be found
in the unspoken whispers of her eyes
casting out spells on the night.

Let her love be my salvation;
her silence my resurrection,
for in her lies the truth.

Mother of Water and Salt
By: Meadow-Lark

Coffee steam stirs with
salt tossed by bubbling
fingers through the air.

Bipolar moon desires
the ocean, chaining it's
body to the sand, then
pushing it back again.

Filtering sand from
their cavities, large
radius polyps pose a darker
green than the blur of
conifers flowing by the
backseat car window.

Rain is our notebook's reaper,
but it's ingredients provide shelter;
they are not bothered by it's
tapping against closed stomata.

Sea lions open the drunk
flask of sunlight and argue in
absence of the wet buffer.

Hermit crabs and hermit people
look beyond their mantle and
push their red fingers beyond the shell.
They admire the twilight as
rain washes it away, the ocean returning
to its lover.

The pale surface remains, where you
can yell, confess, cry
and see nothing but a saline mother
shifting otoliths of sand,
and listening.

Hummingbird
By: Michaels Ink

Little Hummingbird
You flutter here in the air
Bringing joy to all

Spring's Encore
By: Mindful

Oldies remain great
long after summer's encore.
Sticky sweet songs
of those humid summer nights
remain long after autumn's encore
finds technicolor fans
pressed into the fabric of earth,
reborn from decay
into the reunion tour
of the coming spring.

A Keeper
By: Mmmmoon Lion

A fingers touch we often take
Silent emotions sweet as cake
Left upon your lips for me
I want you for eternity

Without words we understand
In acceptance not reprimand
With eyes that launch a thousand ships
Desire grows beyond your hips.

It's you it's true I always knew
Magnetic movements in the night
My monsters grew yet still you slew
Dark fears beyond the dawns first light.

The Oak in The Blizzard
By: Mr. Q

My boots creep one two claws that scrape
shoelace deep into fuzzy Bahama sand
before cracking on frosted marble.
Toes behind melt and lift into mist.

Wiley Jack tugs at my jacket. Wound snug,
he squeezes with cold blood as cotton dust
falls from above.
My four paws become two behind a wall.

Familiar tapered fingers shoo the fluff
as a wrinkled back raises the coils up
on knobbed knees that sink to the
bottom of the sea foam.

I eat the air, embers light,
wheels churn,
and the glad grey
feeds me coal.

But Jack pulls my left,
Toes slip back into dust
and black peers out
the strata face, hungry.

Grandfather rumbles, shoulders fall, grains drip,
and bury him to the waist. My right pushes in aches
My left struggles free, wheels turn as papa explodes
and stands as he holds me on his stump.

How Does It Feel
By: Mrslilboo

Being without you is like
a wound that won't stop bleeding
An infectious yearning
wanting & needing
Like a band aid being ripped off without any warning
Like last call on Sunday
night at 2 in the morning.

Like a hollow hole in the ground that's infinite
Like wearing out your "good" sweats that no longer fit
Like your boss yapping on
and on endlessly
Like a stubborn lock that
won't open without its key.

Like a Hail Mary pass with the
game on the line
Like a dying friend who's running out of time
It's like when there's no toilet paper left when u already sat down
Like when everyone says "cheer up" when all u wanna do is frown.

It's like bad days when nothing ever goes right
It's feeling for your side of the bed every night
It's the projects you just haven't gotten to just yet It's the taste of their lips that
you will never forget.

It's the mile long weekly to do list
it's blowing out the candles but never getting your wish
It's like trying to stay as busy as possible with this or that
It's the constant feeling of this monkey on your back.

It's like a criminal holding you against your will It's the empty space in my
heart that only YOU can fill
It's your part time job weather you want it or not It's being wrapped in your
arms and knowing what I've got.

It's the dreams of "Someday" that you cling to for dear life
It's the fantasy of becoming your future wife

152

•

It's that one mistake that your ashamed of and deeply regret
It's hoping you feel how much I love u and that you never will forget.

It's constant missing holidays and seasonal smiles
It's feeling your here within my heart despite thousands of miles
It's a deserted beach dark and desolate beneath the oceans tide
It's believing we are special and just going with the vibe.

It's the last scoop of your favorite ice cream It's waking up sweating from the
same creepy dream It's a soul crushing need to feel you and
hold you tight
It's like apologizing when deep down you Know your right.

It's the eye of the storm just have to grab on and hold tight
It's tenacity and never giving up without a fight
It's pitch black darkness when u forgot a flashlight.

It's the certainty when you know you have finally found your Mr right
Its seeing it all come to fruition and together leading a happy life.

Mother Nature's Dreams That Come
By: Myriad-Dark

Sleeping beneath an oaken bough
Mother Nature's dreams are spun
All through the night she's dreaming of the sun.

Resting by a mountain stream
Hear her gentle waters sigh
That echoes in her voice with the sound of wings that fly.

Find her in a field of green
Beneath a canopied sun
A gentle breeze through tousled corn an earthly song that's sung.

While she dreams her dreams of Kingdom come...

Angel Came Down From Heaven Yesterday
By: NickO3058

It was just yesterday
when I heard those sweet sounds
floating through time
through youthful forests
of timelessness

The clash, the fury
the harmony,
the glorious expositions
with the full force of being
We lived for that present
We gave it all
to utter exhaustion
left nothing more
until another time
to do it all again

Few have been able to connect
in this world
we melded and molded
weaved and woved
through each other's essence

Few would know the depths of dissonance
we did travel, into the madness unresolved
the other side of life
from symphonies of granite walls scraping
to transposing tranquilly
to cacophony's tension
to triadic tonics of consonance

Tribal essences of lysergic powers
brothers in the ethereal
Cloudy illusions
Succinct sharpness
Forces of mind and matter emitted brightly
produced godly homage
to the burning desires to be one with Ra

Our Rig Veda of mysteries
note by note...tandem melodies
evoking the fates
the butterflies that fade
the sweet smell of passing seasons
death but not the end
of the songs we sang

Thankfulness of those times
I watch as you struggle with ill-borne invaders
sapping light from the soulfulness of your timbre
I am helpless yet hopeful
that we may bounce through the staff
together again
but for just a few moments
before my rhythms
no longer sound
for the horn no longer blows

Reach to the universe
Draw your strength from it's cadence
We will all be a part of it's anthem of suns
Waiting for the sign of the
Dal Segno, my friend
And may we start all over again
at the page the angel of the universe creates
in common time

Your resolution has not sounded yet
There will be another day
to feel the Earth's composition
and we will laugh and spite the fates
once more from the top
the highway never ends
the music never stops

Witch and The Hunter
By: Nithin Bharadwaj

The whole nation was in chaos
They heard about the witch in loose
Forrest was filled with her preys
Witchhunters were set out to chase

Witchhunters were all brave and strong
They had big muscle as hard as rock
Axe in hand all they wanted was
To cut that foul witch in two halves

Days went on their efforts undone
Group of hunters break into ones
One thirsty hunter reached a stream
He found a girl with beaut extreme

hunter forced her to beastly stuff
Soon she showed her true self
She was the witch, protector of the Forrest
You deserve this pain for showing disrespect

She kissed him as he asked her for
His soul left him and reached in hers
She said it's the fate of all greedy men
Only by protecting nature you'll be fine

Visions
By: November Rain

I

I see myself
drifting
in the desert sky

where whirlwinds paint
my portrait in the dust of
my disappearing dreams

and I'm wearing a smile

II

I see myself
floating
in an ocean of blue

where my hopes shimmer
like slowly sinking ships
in the rays of the sun

and I'm sipping lemonade

III

I see myself
crumbling
in a cracked mirror

where distorted views
reflect the frown
of my dying aspirations

and I'm blowing life a kiss

Greyeyes Smith

Bad Company

Sculpted by the Gods
By: Greyeyes Smith

She stands before me living art
Cotton over olive flesh
Raven locks wave to the will of spring breeze
Long fingers glide to brush plump crimson lips

Honey irises call out to be tasted
In sticky sweet acrobatic adoration
Posed to be a challenger to the stars
Her curves and peaks sculpted by the gods

Calling to be worshiped and revered
Inside my Toga virilis
Ambitions no less than Romulus
She is the hemisphere

I will make her my Rome
Conquering her one lick at a time
Under heated whispers
She will be mine

The Myriad
By: Orpheus

High atop The Myriad,
I sail the desert sea.
Ever searching for the soul,
who waits for only me.

Shoreline fathoms rise and fall,
to etch the weathered hull.
Keeping time with lonely cries,
sung out by sandstorm gull.

Winds imbued with silica,
rub raw my hands and face.
In the crows nest calling out,
I search for any trace.

I built this ship with my two hands,
my heart knows every beam.
By night I sail a sea of sand,
by day of her I dream.

Eyes as blue as fabled tales,
of ancient oceans past.
Skin pale as the ivory,
that guilds the wheel and mast.

Hair that rolls in wild waves,
like grains upon this keel.
Summer auburn, winter brown,
the gleam of beach dune seal.

My dreams say I'll have her at last,
pulled close, no need to roam.
I'll tear apart this stem and bow,
to build for us a home.

I named this vessel Myriad,
for all the countless days.
That I will spend a happy man,
held by her azure gaze.

Lascivious Midnight Gambol
By: Orpheus

Salacious tension ripples out,
from bones into the skin.
Igniting on these empty sheets,
as need returns again.

Hunger casts off blankets here,
and issues from my lips.
Writhing in the moonlit glow,
to pulse of phantom hips.

Singe impassioned reverie,
sweet torture of my soul.
Her release is far from me,
two halves that make a whole.

Gnawing on my wicked bones,
each muscle drawn like bow.
Twisting ever fitfully,
in longing's midnight show.

Sweat will soon evaporate,
while on such burning flesh.
Eros' seeds are cast about,
like wheat upon the thresh.

No hallowed sleep will come about,
while need is unfilled.
Consume me in the symphony,
till claim's completely spilled.

I have those broken angel wing eyes
By: Pam Ray

I have those broken angel wing eyes
that can't see beyond
the three shots too many
thrill of you
cradled
in the pit of my stomach

I'm going to sink
a slow burn
of teeth marks
in dry blossom
whispers of hungry flesh

the early morning
of your in the shade touch
awakens
the river coil
of the words between us

both of us wanting
to get lost
in the after the fall artwork
that spills from straitjacket pulses.

every time
the whiskey steam cravings
of our cracked lips
touch
I feel I've given birth
to another part of myself

a tangled branch
taste of the serpent, woman
holding
a sword in one hand
and a need for you in the other.

You Want to Taste
By: Pam Ray

you want summertime
suckled from the peach's
deep blush

but refuse to pit your tongue
against the poison
that winters the shrine
and the crumbling
of your expectations,

there's a clutch
in spreading adoration
into melba toast points
and pomegranate seeds

sabers drawn
to plunder the grace
between the scorn of scorpions,

go ahead fill your belly
with all the marzipan jewels
in your crown

sooner or later
you will vomit the stars
that died at your feet

then who will set
your pinstripe tie
into a gentleman's knot,
and carry you to lunch dates

dirty martinis gulped down
with hookers and God.

The Mountain Poem
By: Papa Terminus

Coming down from the mountain
my thoughts arise
just like the that yellow orb on high
smoking reefer,
sipping on elderberry wine

rushing through the turnstile
I became caught by a high wind
looking down I am centered
my moment to shine
losing track
as months go by
sitting on grassy knolls
reading books by Rowling and King

Coming up the mountain
I heard a humming bird sing
drinking sweet nectar
I pass the joint on the right
everything is zen from where I stand
flying high above the clouds
its just another dreamy acid trip

coming down from my perch now
like a caged bird who sings
Etta James and B.B. King
these blues assault me
as I drift
down past the highways
just a busy bee
watching the world go by

Ode to the Screaming Dragon
By: Papa Terminus

O' scream dragon scream...
like a banshee wailing, outside my window
chase the dragon, down the rabbit hole
techno-colored rainbow flowers, reach
for a lemon yellow sun, lemonade hues

O' scream dragon scream...
spitting fire, smoke billows from nostrils
pretty young maids, tattoo of a black rose
heavy metal flames over the seas, arise
where the great old one, slumbers still

O' scream dragon scream...
hear the minstrel sing, the crown has rolled
the throne is pretty vacant, the jester sits there
like a hyena he laughs, the punchline was told
yet, no one heard the joke

O' scream dragon scream...
spread leathery wings, take flight over the sea
hear the bullroarer greet, claim your defeat
the arrow from the bard's lute, shot
downward spiral you spin

O' scream dragon scream...
the tomes are written, unforgotten yet smitten
like yarn to a new born kitten, tangled web
woven into a tapestry, feeble fingers bend
the flowers cease to bloom

O' scream dragon scream
over the oceans you soar, a natural wonder
the magnitude of beauty, horror
breathing fire, the smell of sulfer arises
like the great Cthulhu opening his eyes

Empty Chair
By: Papa Duck

Brisk night cold and damp
hearth rolls living flame
fire crackles burning coals
shadows dance on window pane

Wooden rocker slowly creeks
sewn quilt wraps and covers
reading lines within a book
glasses tilt down and hovers

Cupped coffee in trembling hands
darkened roast lightly sweet
luring aroma of flavored cream
evenings toast wakening treat

Memories flow like hourglass sand
shifting smile pulls and lifts
silent chuckle from deep within
couples guiles a treasure missed

Drifting back to golden days
loves prime new and strong
life slipped by us fast
clocks chimed harmonic songs

Bowed head from my mourning
soft sigh over lips
deep breath fills lungs
goodbyes terror grips

Wiped eyes of blurred vision
big yawn stretching out
dancing light flashes her silhouette
gaze drawn but with doubt

Empty chair across the room
worn backing from years of use
faded pillows touched by sun's rays
leather cracking springs loose

Basket of wicker lays at her throne
crochet needles and yarns of string
tissue and bible on tables end
left as a tribute to my queen

Her flowered scent teases nostrils
echoed whispers fill the air
bids me a goodnights sleep
as I nod to the empty chair

Daydreams of a Muse
By: Philip Palazzolo

tie up your hair with a gold pin
and tie up all the past sins
I lay my heart to create these meek rhymes
It penetrates through the night and sky
construct bittersweet tenderness
Out of scars of past goodbyes

You see, but raise a pearl-white hand
and let down your long hair with a cry
all the men who have tried are scorned and beat
and sea like foam on the white sand, speaks
while the moon climbs the soul of the sky
Awake but to run into your passing feet.
You whisper softly, fate can't be beat.

Zephyr
By: Phoenix Aradia

I feel you coming before you arrive, making me feel acutely alive;
the air is extra still in anticipation.
Then with a whir and roar you rush in, creating a distinctive din,
and the power you have stretches imagination.

You rattle my bones deep inside, and my feelings start to collide;
somehow soothing and exciting me together.
In a long howl or short gust, you tend to stir up the dust,
and provide lift to the underside of a feather.

Green leaves are snapped, like a whip is cracked;
double-jointed branches are put to their test.
Whole trees sway, up where the squirrels play,
and birds lay eggs in a tiny, twiggy nest.

Down on the ground, your impact is also found,
you pass through grass, like fingers combing hair.
When your cyclones touch dirt, they cause the earth to hurt;
leaving a once lush landscape, stripped naked and bare.

But your softer side is not less, than the most gentle caress.
No more imposing than a sleepy, tranquil breath.
It's what you're able to carry, that can greatly vary;
bringing a freshness in or a contagious death.

Along the Sea
By: P.M. Murphy

if I was just another sunrise
where the water reflects
my morning wakes.
a visual masterpiece
where I gloom best
on a morning after.

would your hands still
cup my waters
when the reflection
doesn't sing?

would you still part ways
with my moons
that circle around me?

would you let your arms
soak in the belly strokes
you give in my sea?

does the cold dark scare you
from everything that is
and encompasses me?

if these questions do not show
the times you have found
the world you seem to think
that my sun rise seems to be,
then let the ocean waves carry you
to another side,
another side of this beach.

You're 'Avin A Giraffe!
By: Podders

We escaped and hid out in a pub
drank the beer there and ate all the grub
at about two am we went homeward again
through the park after drinks at a club.

Now Frank couldn't walk, what a mess
and that's where I have to confess,
I would leave him right there with his feet in the air,
in a remarkable state of undress.

I've tried all I could do in my might
but I'm sure he won't lay there all night,
"Get your ass of the ground, its the lion compound!"
Frank was up and was soon out of sight.

Print That!
By: Podders

Turned out to be true, the printer is new,
the other was powered by steam,
the boss has splashed out but there is no doubt
it's deductable under some scheme.

A printer that works is like having perks
in an office where everythings old,
the typewriter's good when it doesn't draw blood
and the Telex should really be sold.

Shiney and new, "Lets see what you do",
as I tested the printer with Val
"I'm sorry Matt but you cannot do that",
said a voice remenisant of Hal.

The printer's alive! (And a little contrived).
Val and I were quite taken aback,
there on the screen was a face looking mean
so I gave it a technical whack!

I tried the by-pass but the printer's an ass
and blocked me at each tit-for-tat,
in a sight seldom seen Val sat on the screen
pressed a button whilst shouting, "Print that!"

Fraudulent Love
By: Poeta de Cabra

Our love was the greatest
certainly of no equivalent
But, the truth came out
you're nothing but fraudulent

Gave my heart and soul
to the one of my dreams
Wasn't getting the same
in reverse, so it seems

Gave you some freedom
careful not to smother
You took advantage though
lay in the arms of another

Whilst I was home alone
you had the town painted
Out partying with another
seems our love is tainted

Prayers were answered
as my heart beckoned
Could only think of you
every beating second

Gave my all to you
lot of love and devotion
Your acting, had me believing
that you shared the emotion

When I first realized
simply broke down and fainted
No longer can share a love
that is obviously tainted

Hope you are happy now
that my heart's been broken
My love was sincere
yours, was only a token

Nothing was as it appeared
my love, seemingly flawed
Heartbroken, now knowing
your love was totally a fraud

Deceived me with your lies
you were simply a fake
Now all the love I had for you
somehow, I have to forsake

Tidal Pulls
By: Poetic Alchemist

a bashful moon does peek thu curtain's veil
assessing starry-eyed the twinklings that night.
the faded flashlight of lazered cuts, the light
that postal stamps her signature exhale.
the dark's embrace does in its dry attempt
to cloud the journey made of her passing,
shows feel of his daughter's trespassing,
and fully releases his cooling contempt.
a god of time, a watchful hourglassed mind
does sand the beach in oceans of greeting.
does chronos now still at saturn's meeting?
he slows his ticks off in his fated unwind.
these rhythms start their paced moments apart
a pulse now beats in the steady heart.

a pulse now beats in the steady heart
of one who bathes in glows of dancing light.
She who goes clad in Luna's lengthy flight
knows gathered times that passed in witches's art.
an ocean wave is drawn by neap's domain,
expiring, breaking mists of rocky spray.
In timed retreat many gifts will convey
the sea's pleasures in its wandering wane.
the treasures laying in receding wake,
are shelving mem'ries that died in transits.
remains to paint the beach in texture's fits
rendered by hands unseen in frothy break.
the potter designs the animal embrace
of frugal opalescent colored trace

Of frugal opalescent colored trace
is glowing gown that graces Luna's form
that matches step by step her danced perform
in lightest undress of gossamer lace.
the crescent less bold, dance grows old
she hides her self away in clouded disgrace.
The living sun scolds her for final place
in ballets, lovers many, have extolled.

Does Ra and Isis conjoined at day's birth
show matters truest desire, dawning fires
of lovers attired to acquired aspires,
a growing day feeding from mother earth.
the youngster hides in skies beginning pale
a bashful moon does peek thu curtain's veil.

River Flowing, Mountain Growing
By: Poetic Alchemist

The river flows, a heart of torrent in its wake.
Do listen! Wand'ring water's pull does sing medleys.
The mountain grows great as deepening echoes quake.
They sing their songs from buried bedrock and eddies.

A love that's borne, kindled fires birth, is burning stew.
"Ain't no damn mountain higher, any sea this deep,
then the love baby I'm feeling right now for you."
So pull me closer, let's make learning curve more steep.

A touch of airy kiss, a taste of heaven's bliss
carries the sunset's wake into darkening sky.
A lowest groan leaves my lips from this shocking kiss
and I knew life before you taught me how to die

I died in strengthened arms to reawake to view,
in solaced heart was true, a spirit born anew

JHatter

Hatter Unmuted

A Whispered Soliloquy
By: JHatter

For those I trust to carry on
a minute please, this wont take long

Visions drawn with a poets pen
dressed to end then start again

The simple things that walk on by
n'er the time to wonder why

Holding hands that owns the time
gathered words that never rhymed

All things that pass will forever last
they'll lead to where I'll be

Taken down without a sound
in a whispered soliloquy

The window glass where I sat
to paint the skies above

To know its me and that I am free
I leave you all my love

Solar Love and Luminosity
By: Poetic Bella

The vibrancy of the sun, kisses
and brightens the sparkling face of the stars.

The stars in return, reflects
and exudes it's shimmering beauty onto the moon.

The moon on it's fullest day, covers
and charms the sunrays with it's dazzling charisma.

Do Not Whisper Forever
By: Preston P.

What is eternity,
that you should offer it to me?

What youthful naievity
could offer infinity
as if the sweetest song could swoon
distant stars, never leaving June?

To promise such is not fit,
for one day these bodies will quit-
ceasing to know tomorrow.
Forever shall ever be covered in sorrow,
adorned with a stone.

Better sleep
comes to those who no sweet lie keep

A Love Story
By: Raven Blackrose

When I told you
you were mine
until the end
of time itself
and I promised you
that I would never
let you go
you
doubted me.

Still
you would not see
the depth

of my love
for you
truly was
for
all
eternity.

Your heart
you refused me
your love
you gave
to someone
who would never
love you
in
return.

I watched
in silence

as he broke you
and I watched
as you crumbled
and I did

the only thing
I could
do.

I grabbed your hand
and I held it
as I looked
into your eyes
and I let you see
all the love
that was yours
and still
you denied me.

So I held you
as you shed your tears
for him
and I stayed with you
until you
breathed
your

last
breath.

Even then
I did not

let you go
I held on
and I cried
as
my
heart
broke.

I
closed
my eyes

and
I too
breathed
my
last
breath.

For a life
without
your love
I could endure
but a life
without you
was beyond
my
comprehension.

My Playground
By: Reneel1111

I wore your emotions like a crown
east or west or up and down
Each smile and every frown
your sleepless nights became my playground

Never intentions to deceive
being in tune I hoped to achieve
Aching hearts draped upon my sleeve
until that day you took your leave

Deciding it was time to break free
reflective glass stared back at me
Painted pictures so I could see
life's riddles on how I came to be

Searching hidden answers to the whys
determination removing diguises
Tenacity parted dreary skies
a whole new world formed before my eyes

Taken Away
By: Rhymarhyma

Out of all the gifts God gives me every single day
I think I'm just as grateful for what he's taken away...
He took my dad out of my life when I was just one
When he made my mom his ex-wife I guess I became his ex-son
and I never understood how a man could be so cold
and I hoped he died lonely, and I hoped he died old
but now that I'm older and have kids of my own
I thank my dad for showing me not to leave mine all alone
See, he taught me one lesson without even knowing he did
Every kid should have a dad, and every dad should have their kid

I can remember the day like it was yesterday
The first time God took my freedom away
It might have been my first, but it wouldn't be my last
and I'm not sure why I grew up so fast
and I'm not blaming God, because every crime I did was me
but I know it wasn't the me that I was meant to be
It would take a long time before I would finally understand
that I would always slip and fall when I let go of God's hand
Another lesson learned on the wrong side of the track;
A day locked away is a day you never get back

Last but not least, and this may seem trippy to say
I thank you, God, for taking my mother away
For having mercy on her in her hours of sorrow
For ending her days with a majestic tomorrow
For lifting her up when she had fallen down
and for taking her life to spare the life of a clown
If she were still here, I know I wouldn't be
I wouldn't be alive, I wouldn't be free
You love me so much, God, that at first I didn't see
you didn't take her from me, you took her for me...

Finding Carolina
By: Rhymarhyma

A friend of mine asked me "Was it worth it? Was it worth loving her?"

When the nights would bite lonely and leave a tear in her eye
I'm the guy who whispered softly, "Carolina, you can fly..."

I just found out
Carolina died
a one-way ticket
on a one-way ride
She took her own life
from deep inside
Pain is just another name
for suicide

She would always run and hide inside the room that makes the rain/ and then she'd call me and confide a lie that she could not explain/ Contain your raw emotion, kid, go and slow your mind/ Yesterday is far away, don't let today fall behind/ So I'd go and pick her up just so she could feel alive/ and as she'd jump into the car, she'd say "Drive...just drive..."

Just to escape
Carolina liked the highs
Running far away
from all those other guys
Freedom by the spoonful
her arms accept the lies
but I still saw life
behind those cold grey eyes

I needed her far more than I needed breath/ and the closer she got to dying it was I who cried for death/ See, as she was craving peace, I was craving what could be/ She always said I couldn't save her, but she was really saving me/ In-between the highs and lows...the blooming, wilted rose/ I would spend my life defending her, because that's the way love goes

Spin the needle
I remember each track
Brown Sugar plays
A crisscross heart attack
Her final sleep rigged
my heroine fades to black
but yeah, it was worth it
because Carolina loved me back

Inside pocket of her coat
she left a little note...

Dear Michael...It's a new day with a brand new dawn/ and I think I gotta tell ya that I must be movin' on/ My heart screams and it seems it's torn apart at the seams/ Think of me and smile, there's no shame in bad dreams/ I've asked for forgiveness of a past I can't outrun/ so I'll spread my wings and fly to the valley of the sun...I love you...

the time traveler's willow~
By: Rhymedraven

I must have passed these flowers
    a thousand times
going home from work
and work from home
while taking the kids out
and bringing the groceries in

they stood there
  welcoming
me, us and everyone else.
each is greeted
with a scent that bends the neck
    to a graceful curtsy

pink flowers with emerald-green
leaves, scattered on both sides of
    a rustic trail
throwing shade onto passengers
in time, inviting them in
and yet you never see them come out

that day was special,
I stopped and smelled,
followed and gazed
as the trail moved up and
up and up through the hills

not even the most hostile weeds could stop my feet
from walking straight
towards pollen and bees.
that day was special,
and nature knew
as it crawled up my ankles
to comfort me; the ants were here.

that day was special indeed.
a sad and happy day
he died.

and as I carried his burden
        up the hill,
I buried my pain within.

... there, beneath the willow
      a widow prays
   while her traveler of times, good and bad,
            lies in
            dirt and grass.

Morning Mystique
By Ristretto

Morning light, dim but elegant, hidden but powerful
Making its way through the half closed window in a lull
It's the beautiful sun opening his eyes slowly & subtly
Trees shadows dazzling with the slight breeze above the floor gracefully
Morning light, slow but swift, heartless but conscious.

Morning sound, soothing yet stunning, simple yet exciting
Dew drops slipping down from leaves, swaying woods through the wind
cutting
Squirrels lurking, the morning whistle, dogs howl
Mother calling, milkman whooping and the day growl
Morning sound, sliding yet adventurous, lumping yet flashing.

Morning beauty, like a new born child, like a flower bud revealing
The dark clouds paling, the night slowly fading, birds started waving
The light orange sky, the shadowy burrow, happy branches walking on air
The sun dazzles, finding its way from the haze, water shimmering on the lair
Morning beauty, striking like the eyes of a newly turned vampire, roaring like a
furious lion

The wizard's wizardry striking the sky with full flurry
Transforming the night to the magical morning mystique !!!

Connecting nature !!!
By: RNayak

One night, I was busy in dream
Gazed from the corner of my dream

Mesmerized by the view I found
Electron's of beam passing in a tunnel
Light was changing its colour

Within that color I found
A bunch of daffodil

I gazed over the daffodil
Beauty of it tranquillise my dil

Yellow was its color which has fallen
And swept by the east wind

Looking into the wind I saw
Yellow dress Queen plucking those daffodil

Her beauty was matching with same daffodil
Forming a relation of her with that yellow flower

She sat in the wood of log
Taking the daffodil in her neck

Inhaling the essence of the flower
Like a nector she was the butterfly

Playing and dancing with daffodil's I gazed
And saw a chemistry between girl and flower

Like a necklace look beautiful in the neck
She took that flower on her breast

She walk to shore and drink mountain water
While decorating flower on her hair

Round round clip of daffodil she makes
And sprinkle firmly over her daffodil hair band

I gazed from the mountain of cave
Suddenly she flipped back and saw me

She told me O king! what do you want
I said O Queen! I want a hut to live near a daffodil land...
Wake up! buddy wake up! Are you not getting late for office today,
While sleeping I said let me remain in dream I am connecting nature....

Curse of the Raven
By: Robert M...

In these halls my father stood, his tacit temple of earth and wood,
often delving into the mysteries of long forgotten lore-
He wrote obsessively of a bird, who muttered, repeated a single word,
but for years his claims had gone unheard...
About the demon who perched above his chamber door;
The ebon, fiendish aberration who frightened him to his core-

Whom the hells had dubbed as "Nevermore".

Surely he had no way of knowing, of the child that at distance growing,
was a product of seeds he'd been sowing,
amidst the days he would explore-
A time when he was not secluded, his darkness not as deeply rooted,
nor was his mind as warped, convoluted
as the fate that was in store.
For merely a shadow of my father, was I able to adore

Which fueled my longing, evermore.

How I wish my father had known, he had a daughter to call his own,
then maybe he wouldn't have felt as alone...
after the loss of his beloved Lenore-
Writhing in his ceaseless sorrow, often a heart he'd wish to borrow,
but despair had met him on the morrow,
just as faithfully, as the days before
Seemingly he was a slave to the misery he bore...

Merely a shell, and nothing more.

So I've come to this dreary place, to find an inkling, or a trace,
of what sped his agony's destructive pace...
wounding a heart, that grief had tore-
What malevolence could instill, to break the broken further still?
Taking the remnants of a shattered will,
and tossing it to the nightly shore;
tearing further the wounded heart he wore.

All to the echoes of "Nevermore".

In this vast and elaborate room, is where the madness would consume,
binding father to his wretched gloom,
til' the dirge of prudence hummed it's final score.
Below the bust that is now broken, there lay an ominous ebon token,
perhaps of the fabled creature spoken...
In the ramblings of my father's lore-
The tortured musings of his tragic inner war,

That left him altered, evermore.

With the grasping of the feather, great evil seemed to tether,
invoking whispers from the nether,
that had soon begun to roar.
Merely a singular blackened plume, emanating a hellish fume,
seemed to summon the herald of doom...
that had defiled these walls before;
The infernal abomination that sat above the door,

Spewing it's credence of "Nevermore".

But with confidence now shaken, fear began to swiftly awaken,
wondering if I were mistaken-
in rapping on hell's edacious door.
The ebony clock let loose a toll, that shook me to my very soul,
then the feather turned as hot as coal,
and fell upon the dusty floor;
Just what grim, ghastly perversions are there in store?

Heightening curiosity... even more.

But as I sat engaged in guessing, with fear and wonder coalescing,
I could not help in expressing,
The inquiries held at my core...
"What of the fiendish Raven... Who took this home as a new found haven,
with image so aptly graven,
in tandem with that of Lenore?"
The creature which forsook the memories of Lenore-

Defiling them, forevermore.

Yet, my echoes wandered about, beginning to fill me with some doubt...
and just as I was about to shout-
The clock again tolled, much louder than before.
Then the door had flung agape, dislodging every silken drape,
and the shadows took the haunting shape,
of the fiend that I abhor;
The one being for which my hatred does outpour-

That flaunts it's name as "Nevermore".

In the Raven loftily flew, as the wind and rain savagely blew,
in this wicked storm that seemed to brew,
in only the merest of moments before.
He made his perch upon the chair, as if somehow he belonged there,
nonchalantly preening, without a care...
nursing the beguiling visage he wore,
carelessly tending... to the mocking disguise it wore-

fueling my contempt, even more.

"You traverse the twisted nether, with evil ingrained in every feather,
not even lending a care whether,
someone stood here as you glided o'er!"
"Detestable demon from the abyss, where the harps of angels have gone
remiss,
still your pride and answer me this...
Why hast thou tainted the sacred Lenore?
the angel, who caused my father's heart to soar..."

But only silence, and nothing more.

"Damnable wretch!" I exclaimed, "With your hubris and pride enflamed,
the fiend who is so aptly named,
as the infamous "Nevermore"-
But as I spoke it's curs-ed name, its eyes seemed to spark aflame,
it flapped its wings and then came,
a terrifying and violent roar,
sealing shut the enormous mahogany door,

Then just stared, and nothing more.

A smell of Sulphur filled the air, its eyes continued to fervently flare,
I was then overcome by a despair,
that I had never felt before.
The temperature rose by many degrees, bringing me panting to my knees,
and as I knelt there saying "please!"
I saw a shadow upon the floor...
cast from the eyes, that burned as molten ore,

That frightened me to my very core.

It was then that I knew, the fiendish devil that loftily flew,
which toted plumes of the darkest hue,
was the man I grew to adore...
My father's soul was to dwell, in this harbinger's corrupted shell,
til the ebon clock's final knell-
could free him from the pain he bore,
The foul, ghastly, gaunt, and ominous masque he wore...

That now will bind him, nevermore.

So now this wicked, malevolent bane, a thousand lifetimes worth of pain,
damning me to spitefully remain,
until these days become that of yore.
Burdened with a baleful dread, the scorn and resentment of many dead,
their sins are cast upon my head,
just as was said in father's lore;
now a vile specter, damned to walk the nightly shore-

I am doomed to wander.... forevermore...

Inescapable She Sees Things Revealed
By: RolinSton

Hoping all of her was good enough

she was not afraid to spill into emptiness

not afraid of splitting apart into nothing but darkness... .

lonely as before

it seemed to comfort her.

Perhaps bliss is adaptable.

Vibrations swirled-patterns

encounters of random

wanting to resist optics
leaning out her windowbox in the morning
her habits blinked into atoms.

She sees things revealed
but needed something real... .

life didn't understand her the way she did.

Were you ever as happy in flesh and bone

in the weight of dimension ?

Smiles cannot predict results

you walk like a frightened stranger
trembling and shaking.

Is it fair and reasonable to be afraid ?

I can stay another night if you like.

She leaned out her windowbox
sinking into perpetuity with more disbelief

because it was reachable... .

knowing somewhere else is a better place to hide.

Cheryl Wilcox

Andi, Cheryl, Mindy, A Notebook and A Pencil

Yesterday's Echo
By: Cheryl Wilcox

i

Today,
your ghost carves
me out of the shadows
I stand in your presence
and bear the weight
of a thousand broken yesterdays.

I hold onto the shirttails of
light as it slips through
my fingers and falls beneath
tomorrow's cracks and.
shiver in the echo of its chill

to remember-

ii

I remember

the iciness
of your stare,
the way your eyes
burned a hole deeper
than a dagger through
my back.

I cannot smother
the flames that
swallow me
in a flashback or

the fiery truth.

iii

I remember
all of those times
you closed your eyes
and counted to ten,

not in frustration or impatience...

but a mantra and a prayer;
to do away with me.

iv

Today, I gather the cinders
until my own hands are
blackened in guilt.

I look at the ashes
and wish

I had been buried at sea.

Light of Days Yet Unseen
By: RolinSton

To bargain with margins along the wind
you'll need the phosphorous yellow... .
are we to trust the infinite ?

I find aching stars and shudder at their force
shivering by my side, they contain space and time
vapor-steam in the nectar-scheme of things
and most humans do nothing
remaining as novacaine
in the light of days yet unseen.

Will destiny find tomorrow ?
I'll carry my own agenda into millennium
'cause a rocketeer knows time is but a wrinkle
with less pretensions
closer than most want to admit
as the foundry flames this universe
a sunspot carries the many whys
and yet, cannot my planets be counted ?

Space blinks. I ask the Father of Darkness

did I live too dangerous ?

He replied, carry your phosphorous.

Wetland Birds Wingtip to Water
By: Ryan Hunt

wetland birds wingtip to water
brown grass turns green
and the jack rabbit
hops across
rolling hills and dead tree bridges

blue sky and cumulus wisps touch
the tale of horizons
speaking stories
of winter forgotten and summer heat

sun dappled estuary
surging with ground squirrels
secret stash
reaches out green leaf finger tips
toward a tomorrow already grown

sky on fire in the evening
leaves the day under mud blankets
by the side of the freeway

the tap of fingers on keyboards fades
calendar appointments canceled
and the chirping and chattering
of small friends says to
breathe spring and gifts of kindness

Ocean Kisses
By: Rydwichi

an outline of uneven scarlet
circles of painful pleasure
trail their way farther down
to southern peaks
of glory and mesmerisation

while fingers trace veins of gold,
plucking gems from caverns
undiscovered
and worshipping them
with the tips of praying hands

solace in the silk of brushstrokes
over velvet plains that roil
with earthquakes uncontrollable,
the cause deep within

pillars of ivory stand in full glory
as they continue their
exploration for hidden treasures
and sacred sites

the rolling plateaus only increase
with the touch of violence
in a midnight storm
crashing., skewed views
of something glorious
to behold in orbs of ocean blue
and gems of emerald

the waves rise to their full height
and then gravity brings them
crashing down
the effect catastrophic
in the most divine way

the sighs of the ripples
seem miniscule after
the storm resides
but the power still
lingers underneath.

Soaring...!
By: Saikoo

A broken harp!
Shunned by the song of life,
Oh, thee got a candle to flicker
And go out,
Trickling onto the wind,
Thine music now.

Words shall get omitted,
Though born in peace,
At times to flatter,
Honestly it let the maker
Go crazy.

No worry about their beauty,
Azure to ocean floor,
Everything is in tune,
Hidden strings entwined each other,
Knitting the spirits,
A poem lives every here and there.

Calm down for a while,
And,
Listen their humming,
Let the chest beat where everything is
Music,
And peace will be in thine rhymes.

The Breeze
By: Sambit K P

The ocean around that island
where she lived seldom calmed down.
The island itself was almost never visible
to any living eye, except perhaps
to those November birds on their way to winters.
It was always misted over with fine salt spray.

A tiny uncharted island of sand,
a little patch of grassy earth and
that old, twisted and gnarled oak,
which had no reason to be there, but still was!
She was thankful for it though,
for its branches were her home.

Every morning she would leave just at dawn
to visit the little kids on an island a few hours away.
Just for a few minutes she remained there
basking and warming in the midday sun,
before she turned and returned
back to her own oak, her own island.

It seldom rained where the kids lived,
but every day they smelt its hope in those minutes.
For every day, the breeze would collect
the heady petrichor off her salt dampened
patch of grassy oaken earth, and fly it across
those ocean hours, as a beacon of a promise to be kept.

Her Fingers Dance
By: Sam Sampson

Like dewdrops hanging softly from naked branches, her pearls reflect.
Around her neck, nacre necklace drapes softly down, melted jewels.
Her fingers dance, tracing each seed as if to remember.

Following the leaves from the Trees
By: Sam Wise-Aspie

There I lie in my crib as a baby I was drawn to
and brought up around trees, how my dad always
told me to nurture mother nature to embrace it!

Taking me back throughout my younger days
of building bases with friendly faces being
able to climb up branches to reach answers
in such high places!

Walking through my woods with my dog
Lola listening too the sound of the wilderness
looking out for what could be found.

I felt so bound to this as I suddenly heard the pound
of a drum, startled by this I started to follow
the source, Lola caught up with the scent of
it, where ever this would take me was it meant
to be for me...

I thought of all the possibilities of what it could
be until I felt such an energetic vibe, looking
around the corner I saw a kinetic like warp,
standing still there for a minute as I just gawk
at this founded specimen!

Lola takes a dive through it while I strive forward after her,
falling to the ground coming out the other
side calling Lola as I find her waiting for
me by a tree.

Looking up to the skies realizing I was in
a rain forest. What could be in here to
forage, plucking up the courage to explore.

What were the chances of anything living
amongst all of this, willing and digging
for answers I may find!

Strolling on, involving myself in this,

my senses feeling like there evolving
some how trying to adapt to any set
trap. Brushing past vines carefully,
this was a place you couldn't go rushing.

What sort of guidelines were I supposed
to follow, stopping in my tracks I hear
something rustling in a bush telling Lola
to shhh, thrusting itself out at me in a
pounce a cougar was on me, Lola fought
it as she caught it off guard but was
this enough!

As I just thought I'd had my final snuff
something happened from my rear, a spear
struck through the air, stuck in the cougar
hard it must have been stricken with quite
some altitude as it no longer could put
up a fight. It's sight of life finished as
well as diminished!...

Lying there as still as statue so full of
gratitude, something had been my
saviour, someone had done me a
favour, but who and what had got
to me in such a precise period of time!

Gradually rising up to my feet I saw a
black man covered in tribal like markings
with a feeling in me driving me towards him.

Trying not to stare or glare he stood
there still with a knife tied around his chest
made of bamboo as well as a pot with
satchels full of god knows what, he stood
there signalling me to come closer!

I did not know whether this was a test, so
shocked my mind could not rest, pacing
towards him he suddenly shot off racing.

I shouted out "hey come back" and quickly

bolted off after him, Lola by my side keeping
up the pace, where was he running too, was he
taking me to some sort of safe place.

Ducking, diving and shooting past tree's
pushing myself through branches. Fighting
the purge of the sunlight trying to blind my
sight, feeling the urge and surge of adrenaline
within me.

Running so fast with haste to keep
up with my mystery guy nor was I going to
be shy. Getting closer to him I felt the drum
beat pound inside my head the same sound I
heard that had brought me here.

As the trees and everything around me
opened up into a clearing with camps and
huts set up in trees, now I knew that I'd
finally reached my destination.

Looking up high there were platforms and there
was many sorts of man made ledge's one
after the other, now this is what I called
living life on the edge with a lot of
privileges, a community building so
many bridges.

As I came to a gradual halt the man spoke
telling me his name was Emmanuel and
that he was a shaman. Emmanuel had grey
blue eyes, you could tell he had plenty of stories.
So many bracelets dangled in the wind off his arms.

Elaborating more
he said "We have long waited for you
Samuel to come to us, you have so much
heritage in us. We have watched over you
for so long, now we know you are strong and
now you must come and show us your true
faith and beliefs to become one of us. Now you
must control your nerves and calm them,

don't fill them with alarm! Do not worry
about your dog my people will assure you
that she is kept safe".

Setting off with Emmanuel I soon found that
they all believed from the trees they could
harness great energy, they were sacred to
them, after finding out all this I finally
understood everything with all my questions
answered.

Emmanuel spun around grabbing his
pot and one of his satchels grinding and binding
some powder up, soon realising as Emmanuel
combined his mixture I could feel the drum beat
gradually getting louder with great power.

Emmanuel rotated round now facing me telling
me "You will now face mother nature by testing
the water with your faith and noble grace!"..

As soon as he said that final word he blew the remedy
out of his pot into my eyes, I sent out such sharp
cries as my sight faded then I remembered what
he had stated to me about how I should react and act.

Taking my hand he told me "Come I shall take
you to where you need to stand then you will
understand what will make you a greater man!"..

Guiding me through taking me on some sort of
path, nor did I have a clue what he could be hiding
from me, biding and defying my emotions with
a gut feeling in me that I knew I may have to
switch what senses I feel off.

Plodding on up and over tree roots, getting
pulled through tree shoots as Emmanuel says
"We are nearly there, take a deep breath and
fill yourself with this pure fresh air!".

While in the background I start to hear a silent yet

trickling sound, it felt familiar and so similar like a flow of water that soon
started to alter getting heavier!

The remedy in my head trying to evaluate my
fears trying to elevate it as we get nearer our
location, feeling the beckoning reckoning call!..

The terrain getting steeper the crashing sound
of water getting deeper. My eye sight re-awakening
from this blindfolded state from the remedy, gazing
at my new surroundings there I ' am on the top of a
waterfall stood on the edge of a rock ledge!..

Emmanuel saying "You may set yourself straight and
now you must take what we call the leap of faith, this will see if you are
worthy of your mark!"...

Taking a little glimpse from the top of the waterfall
to the bottom, seeing some chimps in a tree trying
to tease me with there mockery.

I felt like my heart was going to stop after I soon worked out that it was about
a two hundred foot drop, shuddering Emmanuel ushering me on assuring me that
I will be all right.

My body was buzzing with determination as well as such thrill with no chill of
nerves and that's when I found that this was meant to be!...

Taking a stride back enough for me to go at
an even pace. My feelings neutral at an even
tide, taking a run up I race off and dive off
the waterfall.

Free falling as I feel the air calling and pulling me down so fast, feeling
graceful also faithful! My face gently hitting the water as I brace myself for the
impact with every part of me still in tact!...

Emmanuel waiting for me at the bottom, long had I forgotten what it felt like
to have a moment like this where you really felt like you are living your life. Those
are the moments that are always worth chasing for!

Approaching Emmanuel he spoke

"You did that with such pride now you have
earned and deserve your prize! Come we
must take you to Aunnel for your initiation
and celebration!"...

Arriving back at camp, thriving too see what
this would all be about. Emmanuel taking me
to Aunnel as we enter his hut.

Emmanuel introducing me to Aunnel saying "This is
our ritualist he will give you your mark only
you will be able too see it, now are you ready
Samuel for your ritual this is something we
take seriously so don't ridicule it!"...

Aunnel taking my arm telling me "I mean no
harm by this but we need a little for sacrifice"
and with that Aunnel nipped my arm with a
knife as he let my flood of blood drip into
his pot as my wound soon quickly starts to
clot.

Taking a sip of my blood out of his pot
he says too me "Your blood has a great length
of strength in, with mine combined it will define
your mark and bless you with such a shrine full
of wisdom!"...

Adding a few dried leaves and seeds he believes
would fill me with such great beliefs, soon after
he starts humming, focusing numbing out everything
else around him, aiming all his energy at his pot as it
soon starts flaming!

Smoke surrounds the ground as he
shouts chants out to his lost and found ancestors, no
time for the restless only for wrestlers so you could say that have there way to
tackle and topple
anything against nature!...

Looking down at my arm locked on to it
as if it was a target, I was entirely shocked

as I watch my mark form in this ritual storm,
I felt so drawn and sworn to this like I'd been
reborn!

As everything came to a gradual halt
Aunnel gave me his pot and told me "To
complete your mark you must inhale and hold
back the remaining smoke this way you will
be gaining your own skill that you will be able
to draw power from within the trees!"...

Deeply inhaling the smoke, holding it back as
I feel it spread around my body and embed it's
thread in me with my genetics and ethics changing.

I wondered what skill in me I was unveiling would
I be a warrior with the will to kill no matter how
much blood has been spilt or a shaman stopping
anything wilt from nature or could I be some sort
of hybrid led and taught to learn both ways nor
would I kid about this!...

Aunnel telling me "Now your mark is formed
the more it will grow when you show to nature
a good deed to protect it against the living and it
will reward you with great skill and power that you
may shower against anything that may try to harm nature, nature can be a
great creature in its own way!"...

Getting up that next day with Lola feeling so
free up within my own tree, I was now known
as a tree walker, a stalker in the dark taking
anything out that may lurk around the corner!

A smirk on my face more than ever, never had
I wanted to endeavour in a world so much as this.
Emmanuel meeting me giving me a speech telling
me that if you wish to stay here Samuel then there's
no need to preach about it to me, with that choice
given to me in my hands. I listened to my rightful
voice coming to a decision quickly with no decisive
incision against it.

Making up my own ten commandments I
swore upon them. I would keep and make
such a great demand on them to leap forth
when a challenge arises no matter what sort
of disguises it may be in to fool me.

I would be there when ever my people need it, a call
away to pull back what ever lingers to where
it came from, shut tight against its own darkest
hinges, kept well contained as well as restrained.

Then with that given time I'd never stop being
trained, for each day I would have gained a different
sort of element to use that I could learn to control.
This is what I now yearned for and earned, awoken
with a great well spoken companion...

Cocklebur Canticle
By: Sand Painter

i

The clinging cocklebur annoys the hare
who doesn't want the spherical freeloader
hitching a ride on his bushy tail.
The seed's spikey, tan travelbag
crosses the wild field on the hare's flank.

ii

The farmer comes in from the field and pulls
burrs from the laces of his boots.
He hears his wife setting plates on the table.
Deaf from birth, she's made her way with silence.
When she sees him come in, her hands sign
with fine movements, composing words
for his savvy eyes. After supper
he signs that it's time to dress for the concert.

iii

At the concert their daughter's hands
play a journey through sound.
Her fingers dance on the keys,
travel across ivory to unravel the melody,
like the cocklebur giving up it's seed.
With the audience's standing ovation,
her mother stands too and applauds.
She feels the auditorium tremble
from the soles of her sapient feet.

iv

As they return home in their red pickup,
they watch the rabbit in the moon
crossing the night sky.
And there's the cocklebur
riding on the rabbit for free.

Freight Train
By: Sarah Gosa

freight train
under thunder clouds
windows chatter

There is a soup bowl
in my old home town.
Some make out like Spring's
a fancy lady with dainty daffodil drawers
but I know she's a big fat slob
wearing moldy coveralls.
With a pocket full of gumdrops
she'll plop her muddy boots up
anywhere she pleases
and wipe her sticky fingers
all across your lawn.

Evo-motion
By: Scarlet Victoria

embody the fluctuating edge
waterfalls of universal wear and tear
unfold origami-asms of rainbow prisms
reflecting me
projecting you
right angles
chime
for
hourglass sundials
blow sand tornados

let us play

school

together...

Faucet Dance
By: Scarlet Victoria

Waterbeds strike from showerheads
like starved snakes on wildfire sands
unto famished unchained sage oil skin
lathered in sandalwood steam
formed by a subway speed moan

hearts flutter electric wings of molten ice
swirls of vision-squeezing silhouettes
stroke twitching Modena muscles
trigger pressure-pulsing toes to curl
over stitch-kinked tabletops

eyelids twinkle
licked lips squeal
shadows dance over omenta keys
a whip cracked maiden
her breaths are his domain
muted by minted smacks
backside marks of 'mine'
in
1,
2,
3,
waxed hand-whacks...

dominate
detain the inmate
oint the alabaster tub
in mirrored headlight sighs

before...

key to lock click snap an ear

briefcase daemon
announces a baritone "I'm home"
creaking staircase plunders
footsteps run

thud tap tap
thud tap tap
thud tap tap...

Oubliette
By: Silk BlackRose

why do you spin
such glorious webs
in the requiem of my madness

where all light
has faded from stars
that died millennia ago

be it thee are woven of stardust
by some forgotten gods palm?
now fallen from grace
whispering in the ears
of wretched mortals?

why dost thou torment me
as if every line were a lock
and a word, the key
to set my spirit free

is it the way
silver moon sways
the flow of my poet's hand
brushing your galaxies
across the void of a page

or is it the way
my darkness tastes
on the tip of your velvet tongue
that holds thy fancy?

Lady,
thy waltz beneath my blackened shroud
inflames a beating as of symphonies,
singing arias and dirges,
crashing in a riot of cacophony

parting silence's veil
to pour your blood
into my inkwell

while my fingers caress
the song of your voice
across the aged parchment
till, at last, my demons weep

After the Storm
(Opus 4 - Love for another)
By: Silly Boy Blue

If I could harness the colours of the wind,
and lay them at your tired, weary feet,
tied in bouquets of radiant bloom,
could you embrace the beauty of your life.

If I captured the love in a new-born's smile,
and painted it tenderly with gossamer feathers.
on your sculpted, tear stained, apple cheeks,
would you forget the hurt that fuels your tears?

If I could bathe you in light from a galaxy of stars,
and dress you in the warmth of eternal sun,
shielding you from the biting cold of your reality,
would it cast the frozen midnight from your soul?

If I could pour calming oil on the raging ocean,
silencing the tide of your restless anxieties,
guide you inland, to the safe harbour of my love,
could you rest peacefully in the solace of my arms?

Andi

Andi, Cheryl, Mindy, A Notebook and a Pencil

She Is Listening
By: Simon Guest

An ear pressed against a wall,
Listening,
Tick, tock, tick, tock.

A petal falls gracefully
Upon a stormy ocean.
Waves crash upon ravaged rocks.

Hell hounds pull upon a collar,
Finally freeing a line of small broken bones.
Laughter ensues.

Her eyelids fluttered.
A tsunami rises
Encapsulating a pause in time.

Blackened faces remember.
Chords demoralize.
Tears fall into an overflowing cup.

A child shipwrecked,
Cap in hand,
A saviour launched upon a footstool.

Death is here,
A mutant upon a hill,
Forever listening.

Magical phenomenon
By: Sindhu selvi

You have the color of shiraz
Cuts like a filter paper
No regular looks
Is it a burgundy red or orange or yellow?

Maybe it's a chlorophyll breakdown
OR
Winter's rest
Or
Magic of anthocyanin pigment.

Whatever it may the reason
Whatever maybe the science phenomenon

But you really look awesome
I call its
Nature's way , perfect
Just perfect and beautiful.

Raining from a White Rose
By: SouLProbe7

I may push you away
As far as my fingertips
So my heart won't ache
For a closer embrace

I may tell myself
It's easier this way
As my mind wanders
To a hiding place

We are both honorable
With all due respect
Yet when the rain arrives
Day-dreams do drift

Hands then cupped, gently
Watering the butterfly
As her colorful wings
Paint my palms of prayer

It is comforting to know
The pensive songs of you
Will Forever echo as petals,
raining from a white rose
raining from a white rose
raining, from a white rose

melinda owen

Instrumental Heart
By: SouLProbe7

We should never forget
what it feels like
to be innocent as a child.
The very first time tasting, smelling,
believing, wanting, kissing
obtaining those moments
with butterflies, excitement,
hopefulness and dreams.

To drive a car
for the first time alone,
with the windows down
and your favorite song
serenading your soul.

Music is my warm blanket.
Memories
woven with the strings of a guitar
skin of a drum
ivories of a piano
and frayed around the edges are notes
blowing in the winds
skipping across the ponds
floating down the rivers
splashing into the depths of my soul's contralto.

melinda owen

Nature Welcomes Me
By: Streambed

I wrote a fairy poem this morning,
for the first time in a long while.

It felt good to stretch my wings,
and to fairies, you know
singing is so easy.

Afterward,
I walked out into the back garden,
across the rain-kissed grass.
I stood on a stepping stone
beside the grape arbor,
and felt something settle on my arm.

Surprised,
I looked down and found a broken-winged butterfly
looking for respite.

I blessed it in prayer,
and watched it flutter away
against the shifting sky.

Between the Whitewash
By: Sweet P

Wet white paint spatters
on old blue jeans which have witnessed
this act of renewal across the
planks of this old wooden
picket fence before

Arthritic knees slowly raise
as the smell of memories
flow through an old man's eyes.

Wildflowers he called them
Wild children she had for him
and with time they both grew

Johnny Jump up's, Crimson clovers,
Forget-me-nots, Morning Glories,
and Black-eyed Susans grew along
Black-eyes, baseball gloves with
bats that went rat-tat-tat
along the picket fence line
Where water fights and Soldiers Forts
played where only Sun Flower
eyes could find them

The winds screamed and the fall of
a little nest and baby birds were
softened by flowering peonies
a kitten found in between the posts
tangled in the Vinica vine
tea-parties on the garden's edge
mudpies made and names of colors
learned as Dahlia's bloomed

Her hair was long and her body young
this is how he saw her through the decades
tending children and flower gardens

Spring swept in with new soil,

and boxes by the door
pots with green sticks claiming
the inches of soil still
found in the shade or sun
A pair of old blue jeans, a gallon of white paint
with a note telling him what to do

She saw him coming up the walk and smiled
the old man smiled back and wiped his tears
and understood the beauty of life
between the whitewashes

Life at Speed
By: The Fire Burns

We shoot across the galaxy,
riding the comet's tail,
thousands of miles an hour,
leaving a shining trail.

Stopping here on earth,
for a hundred years or less,
leaving a scar on hearts,
for life is such a mess.

Touching other souls,
sending them reeling from the collision,
just like an asteroid impacting satellite,
controlled with imprecision.

So leave your mark while you're here,
because remember time goes too fast,
then once again into the universe,
our time on Earth never lasts.

The Honed Edge
By: The Fire Burns

We walk the knifes edge every day,
a balancing act that threatens
to cut us apart, down the middle,
one side lunacy, the other sanity.

The fun and most exciting of us,
sit on the edge and dangle our feet
off the side of lunacy.

Wondering just how far out,
we can scoot before we fall?

The Wandering Mermaid
By: Gypsymoongal

I love the forest and I love the sea and
I love all that you are meant to be
I love the rose in bud and the rose in bloom
I love the earth that holds her treasure in her womb
I love the trees and their gentle song
I could listen to the forest's melody all night long
I love every flower and how they embrace every bumble bee
And I love the way the trees sway in unison
with the rhythm of their beat in me
I love the wind that blows through every wave
and every ripple beneath the sea,
As I love to feel the ocean's spirit call out to me
I love the rivers and I love the rain
When my feet are kept away from water
my heart feels pain
As every part of nature is every part of me
and I love every single grain of sand and every leaf on every tree
And every bird that has it's own precious song reminds me just how much I
long to dive deep in the ocean
where I belong.....

The Southern Right
By: Thoughts-of-Solomon

now stand so near
such other world,
deep come close
to shallow its skin

huge black bonnet
bearing spangled
individual
tell-tale callosities

tower-like tail flukes
raised ready suspension,
to smash out reports
scattered sprayed
across ocean's surface

slowed deliberate
consciousness spy hops
then dives deeply prepared
for impossible breach -

weight smashing through
from invisible blue

after loafing a while
what sound so rare,
dignity's breath
measured long,
through all fifty feet
so bass and complex vibration

then gifted to meet
as unfathomed thought
prints rich to the mind,
conveyed direct from
this world's largest eye ball

dumbstruck to whale rhythm
time stands more paused,
moments elongated
yet still all too brief

*   *   *

If they can return
with forgiving,
then it must be possible
to find forgiveness for all things.

In One Another's Thoughts
By: Titus

An inspiration from "Of Doves and Daffodils." by AzureRain

2 Sestinas

The daffodils have wilted, some petals float on the water. I am Narcissus, my reflection wains to have outstretched a hand which tugs at the approval the lake holds. I turn from looking at myself, to see the dove has aspired into a beautiful being, not realising it was myself, a shapely form of distortion!

1.

The breeze, which blew abruptly over stems,
display to doves which once were daffodils
disused by manners which left barely laid,
a moment when I froze their trumpets lost;
Concedes to have withheld the extrovert
Doves which have sound sensing an array.

Floating the caress there drifts array,
add matching petals lightly to their stems,
the showing off the white spoke extrovert,
would echoing of featured daffodils,
reminding me of those, of love's youth lost,
has surfaced like do petals softly laid.

The ripples would towards me share what laid,
between us, out of reach that swooned array
sufficient breeze enough to share ours lost,
am I to allocate the side of stems?
To you my sweet encrusted; - daffodils?
Whose spiralling controls the extrovert.

And from the lake shy slowly's extrovert,
who soothes us more directly than inlaid,
the while on grass so fetch may daffodils,
include the pastel shades of those array!
Albeit the idle dreams those so-called stems,
forget; that doves have idled wanton lost!

I edge towards the clearings which have lost,
loves details through the peace, my extrovert
arise, whilst spring evolves protruding stems,
uprising of the once stood all but laid,
seems pity shows abundance holds array,
such stems which show true yearnings' daffodils.

Forever is it spring, that daffodils,
forget that what is time, to have been lost,
in one another's thoughts, does love which stems
their fanfares made from trumpets' extrovert,
as ageless in the way our fates were laid,
upon the edge of whether souls array!

The daffodils have grown since where I laid,
They leave the extrovert of sound array
since doves are now from lost as those new stems!

2.

That what I was about to say conveys,
On land or lake the daffodils and doves
are frequenting more often for our sake,
intrusion; of a kind which tends to part,
a fling of some acquaintance shown as breeze
disturbing what it is of their cavorts.

To honour love which like the lake cavorts,
upon the slow but aiding set conveys;
a "love you", would be met and like a breeze
A show discerning mood from far off doves,
whose silence all too far were shown to part
dividing our attention for love's sake.

For if, should stems be gathered for the sake,
of those whose other triumphs see cavorts
enabled to allow what they're in part;
of anything considered which conveys
the suspect on the ground shown rows of doves
partitions them like wind shields to a breeze!
Their feathers having had escaped the breeze,

sufficient source encouraged for the sake,
of lovers, and the petting sounds of doves
reminds me that they play here, lake cavorts
Too often, eyes widespread in close conveys,
The evidence of languish there in part;

She'd only stay a minute, though to part,
from asking who she was, the spoken breeze
would spend a life time asking more conveys,
for womanhood to mention for the sake,
of others that like daffodils, cavorts,
no end of detailed thrills of courting doves;

Should spirits be to those who show us doves,
to have include those solemn hopes as part,
where I, can pray at least towards cavorts,
or having heard her whisper through the breeze,
where daffodils who blew for kisses sake,
a thereabouts where each took hold conveys.

That far off lands define for which our sake,
would pass that stage cavorts the show of doves,
a breeze from which the sentiment conveys.

We're But Mere Sheep,...So What Else Is New, Ewe?
By:T-stich

You have these thoughts within your head
unfortunately, it's all been said
that's right girlfriend, it's nothing new
somewhere, someone has thunk it too

we're but mere sheep, we're born to follow
each scripted line, each verse rings hollow
that swill you just regurgitated,...
some bard of old most surely stated

so hold the phone, you're not unique
recycled,... all those words you speak
repent, repent,... you do realize
with all you write, you plagiarize

those fancy poems you just rehearsed,
"I'll sue," they claim,.." I wrote them first
I penned them back in sixty four
or something similar, that's for sure"

your brand new rhymes, they're so contrary,
each word, there in the dictionary
oh, woe is you, what will you do?
if you can't think up something new

it pains ewe so, ewe just can't sleep
relax girlfriend,... try counting sheep
it's not that baaaaad, and you can quote,
"I said,..."Don't let it get your goat"

for even if someone has said it,
that doesn't me someone has read it
so write it down, girl, I won't squeal
besides,... sometimes it pays to steal

In fact, ewe may just win a prize
before those experts realize...
"she pulled a Seuss,.. that dirty rat,
she stole the cat out of the hat"

but seriously, ewe, no need to mope
tomorrow's new,... there's always hope
some brand new words may be invented
take back those pents, that ewe repented

for even Shakespeare thought with dread,
"To be or not,...has that been said?"
we all seek answers,...don't I know it
just don't ask me,...I ain't no poet

and disregard my little schtick,..
delete those poems, ewe,... make it quick
before they chance to realize...
ewe cheated, girl,...ewe plagiarized

Slow Dance With Neruda
By: WandaLeaBrayton

I feel your song moving softly,
rippling underneath my skin -
crashing on the shoreline of thought,
raising mountains where oceans once lay.
I taste moonlight on your lips,
falling from ethereal skies of yearning.

As a child,
I watched our cherry trees bloom,
not understanding the fiery blush
that colored my cheeks, soft pink petals of silk.
When Autumn came, the fruit was sweet,
tender juices pouring from my mouth.

Hungered and quiescent under your darkened eyes,
I am a budding branch stretching for sunlight's warmth,
rooted in your earth;
this restless flesh flutters as your fingers
trace edges of wind upon my heart,
every breath we share in shivered silence.

We were born to love this way,
lost in the depths
and found by the tethers of our searching hands
swelling tides in each other's oceans.
Compasses forgotten, we explore the trembling horizon.
I will not be moved, save for the gentle currents
of your water upon my Being.

You reach for me across space and time,
drifting on currents of breath between us.
We lay naked to each other's eyes,
sweetly surrendering to the sea -
unfathomable tempests roar within my blood.

How is grief fathomed, when light cannot be found?
I follow this maddening moon,
laying myself upon you as I offer succor in morning's embrace.

Your hands unveil an artist's touch, sculpting and molding curves,
stroking angles with deftness for colors and lines;
knowing the canvas glides with movements of your brush.
You sketch my love with bold strokes,
redefining the expanse of my borders, of sorrows not quite earned.
We light these sacred candles, wondering why we still feel cold -
flames flicker on the periphery of silence
that will not hold stars as they fall from the sky.

There's a sigh drifting from your lips
that I'd love to kiss into silence, yet, I do not move -
I dare not speak, ending this quiet moment
that stretches between us as an eternity.
I want to feel those gentle hands tangled in my hair, always.

The bud opens shyly,
softly scenting the air with allure
as petals fall gently to the ground.

Leaves stir in a woman
who knows the grandeur of Autumn
and the harshness of Winter, whispering as she waits for harvest...

Such a Beautiful Sound
By: Waynejent

Lay beneath the darken sky
gazing towards soft twinkling stars
reaching my contentment high
horizon teasing with planet Mars.

Quiet night, no commotion
peaceful void, became as one
consumed by infinities vast ocean
thoughtless of the hiding Sun.

Dancing rays from ancient past
windless touch, so perfectly numb
notice the moon slowly pass
nearly lifeless in my vacuum.

Yearning to know nothing more
God's perfection being shown
listen to hear what is life for
only to hear the moon's tone.

Anhedonia
By: WhiteTiger

the morning sky was grey
the sun turned white as the moon
i watered my impatiens and the colors washed away
and music failed to stir emotion

then the face of wonder slapped me
and i knew my dopamine was gone
the neurotransmitters were fried
and i lost desire for sex and love

had spent my lifetime share of highs
long before my death arrived
now just a shell of my former self
a snail's shadow
that inches miles
towards the final finish line
i wished someone would squish me

fated to suffer the contempt of others
who view me as a disease or plague
euthanasia is more humane

a man void of pleasure cannot survive
but doctors never warned me
that the price for killing pain
could lead to years of living death

Piano In The Dark
By: WolfSpirit

she plays piano in the nude
sitting in the dark
i sit and listen to her soul
a sweet, familiar spark

she's making love to Beethoven
in the soft moonlight
as she plays his sonata
and all the notes are right

and when she keys Alicia Keyes
still in state of undress
the rhythm moves my very spirit
in ways i can't confess

i don't think it's her nudity
so much as how she plays
but everything that's beautiful
is jealous of her ways

she plays piano in the dark
her heart is effervescent
and so akin to sweet romance
she's leaving me tumescent

and i would ask on bended knee
her favor, for to play
when she is fingering the notes
my troubles fade away

she plays piano in the nude
the moon and stars are jealous
she captivates the milky way
but never over zealous

she plays my heart..plays my soul
on that baby grand piano
but melts my last ounce of reserve
when she sings soprano

i love piano in the dark
i love my naked vision
for i would walk a million years,
succumb to her derision

she plays piano in the nude
when no one else can see her
the music lifts her heart on high
and only my love frees her

Untitled
By: Writespring88

skies so blue
clouds so puffy and white
looking out the window beyond the horizon
beyond the trees and fields of green
only god him self could create the most beautiful things

As owner of Late Night Poets Room on Allpoetry.com
I want to take the time and acknowledge all of our members.
I appreciate and respect each of you as not only poets but as great people
You are an inspiration to me and to each other.
As the producer of Late Night Poets Radio I want to thank each of you that
listens and participates, without you it would all be for naught.
Huge thank you to all of the Incredible Hosts and Hostesses that create and
captivate you all with their weekly shows.
I appreciate the support of each member that submitted to this Anthology
in support of the radio shows, you are all amazing. Hopefully we will be self
sufficient in the year 2019, along with the possibility for expansion.
I have high hopes along with high ideals for us all.

L..N...P...
By: Fillmyeyes

The most amazing poets
reside in L...N...P
they write they laugh they sing
they're as warm as they can be
we don't take stuff from anyone
we protect what we call home
sometimes, we surely wander
and again we sometimes roam
So many found a home here
away from pettiness and disdain
so we offer out our open arms
to those that seek the same
to those that offer music
I thank you from my heart
to those that offer chatter
so much fun you do impart
for those that offer role-play
you all blow me away
the storylines and twisting plots
make me always want to play
to those that just stay idle
off waiting in the wings
I appreciate you each, and every one
for the poetry you bring
for those that fill the reading list
for all of us each day
I thank you for those gifts you bring
in your tender sharing way
for each of you that comments
taking time to "like" a write
thanks for all the time you spend
from all the poets you delight
for each and every parody
that make me laugh out loud
for every front page pick you earn
I applaud you 'cause I'm proud

keeping all the muse at play
with every contest that you run
I want to thank you all for this
yes each and every one
Now for each and every radio host
from the bottom of my toes
Thanks for all the love you share
with your poetry smiles and prose
but most of all I thank you
for the family we've become
no matter sex, race or country
L...N...P I say "Well Done"

Made in United States
North Haven, CT
31 October 2021

10722336R00152